EGYPT
AND THE
EXODUS

EGYPT
AND THE
EXODUS

by
Charles F. Pfeiffer

BAKER BOOK HOUSE
Grand Rapids, Michigan

First printing, April 1964
Second printing, August 1965
Third printing, October 1967

PHOTOLITHOPRINTED BY CUSHING - MALLOY, INC.
ANN ARBOR, MICHIGAN, UNITED STATES OF AMERICA
1967

CONTENTS

PREFACE

Ancient Israel confessed, "Yahweh heard our voice, and saw our affliction, our toil, and our oppression; and Yahweh brought us out of Egypt with a mighty hand and an outstretched arm, with great terror, with signs and wonders" (Deut. 26:8). Each year at the Passover season Israel remembers God's mighty acts which brought deliverance to a people enslaved by Egypt's Pharaoh. Few people wish to be perpetually reminded of their humble origins, but Israel is ever mindful of the admonition: "You shall remember that you were a slave in the land of Egypt, and Yahweh your God brought you out thence with a mighty hand and an outstretched arm" (Deut. 5:15).

Apart from the Biblical text, however, we possess no documentation for the period of Israel's sojourn in Egypt and her subsequent wilderness experience. The corpus of Egyptian texts is enormous, and scholars try to understand the Biblical events in the light of known facts about Egypt. The reader should be aware of the fact, however, that the Bible mentions no Pharaoh of the Exodus period by name, and Egyptian documents do not mention Israel until she is in the land of Canaan.

These facts do not encourage a skeptical attitude, however, for the events described in the Bible tally perfectly with what we know about Egypt. Many of the Biblical names of the Exodus period — including Moses himself — are clearly Egyptian, and Semites are known to have settled in the eastern Delta region of Egypt in very ancient times. Even the plagues visited upon Egypt have a distinctly local coloring. While contemporary Biblical scholars differ concerning many of the details of interpretation, they agree that at least a part of the people that came to be known as Israel experienced the Exodus.

The covenant between Yahweh and Israel at Sinai forms the basis for an understanding of later Biblical history. Prophets denounced Israel for breaking that covenant, and heralded the day when Yahweh would write a new covenant on the fleshy tables of human hearts (Jer. 31:31-34). The Tent of Meeting in the wilderness gave way to the Temple in Jerusalem, and that, ultimately, to the Word made flesh who dwelt (lit. "tabernacled") among us (John 1:14).

The writer has tried to gather together material pertinent to an understanding of the period of the Exodus in its historical and geographical dimensions. He must leave many questions unanswered, and suggest tentative answers to others. Such matters are peripheral, however. The great redemptive acts of God are clearly delineated on the pages of Exodus, Numbers, and Deuteronomy and the subsequent history of God's people bears testimony to the mighty wonders he has wrought.

Charles F. Pfeiffer

Mount Pleasant, Michigan

EGYPT
AND THE
EXODUS

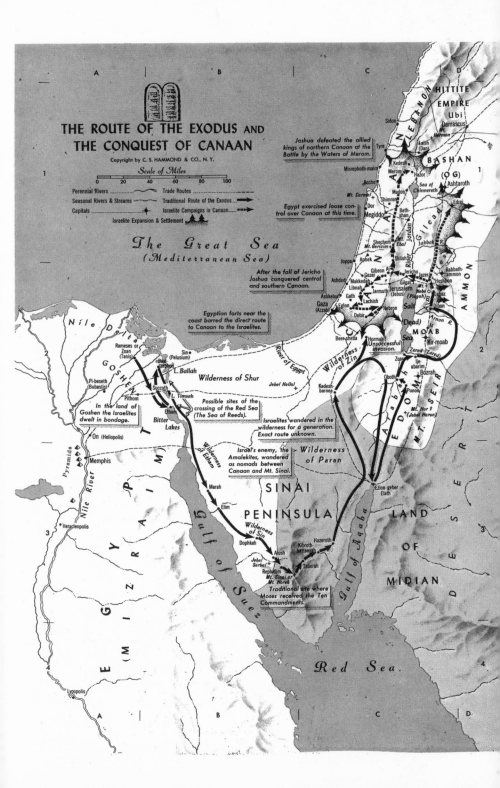

THE ROUTE OF THE EXODUS AND THE CONQUEST OF CANAAN

Copyright by C. S. HAMMOND & CO., N. Y.

Scale of Miles

0   20   40   60   80   100

Perennial Rivers ....
Seasonal Rivers & Streams ——
Capitals ....

Trade Routes ....
Traditional Route of the Exodus ➡
Israelite Campaigns in Canaan... ▪▪▶

Israelite Expansion & Settlement

The Great Sea
(Mediterranean Sea)

Joshua defeated the allied kings of northern Canaan at the Battle by the Waters of Merom.

Egypt exercised loose control over Canaan at this time.

After the fall of Jericho Joshua conquered central and southern Canaan.

Egyptian forts near the coast barred the direct route to Canaan to the Israelites.

Nile Delta

Rameses or Zoan (Tanis)

Sin (Pelusium)

Pi-beseth (Bubastis)

GOSHEN

Baal-zephon
L. Ballah

Pithom

Succoth
L. Timsah

In the land of Goshen the Israelites dwelt in bondage.

Wilderness of Shur

River of Egypt

Jebel Helal

Ethan

Bitter Lakes

On (Heliopolis)

Pyramids

Memphis

Possible sites of the crossing of the Red Sea (The Sea of Reeds).

Israelites wandered in the wilderness for a generation. Exact route unknown.

Kadesh-barnea

Israel's enemy, the Amalekites, wandered as nomads between Canaan and Mt. Sinai.

Wilderness of Paran

Marah

Elim

SINAI PENINSULA

Wilderness of Sin

Dophkah

Heracleopolis

Alush

Jebel Serbal

Rephidim

Mt. Sinai or Mt. Horeb

Traditional site where Moses received the Ten Commandments.

Kibroth-hattaavah

Hazeroth

Taberah

Ezion-geber
Elath

Gulf of Suez

Gulf of Aqaba

Red Sea

LAND OF MIDIAN

LAND OF DESERT

Nile River

Lycopolis

E G Y P T
(M I Z R A I M)

Wilderness of Etham

HITTITE EMPIRE
Ubi

Sidon

Damascus
Mt. Hermon

LEBANON

Tyre

Laish (Dan)

Kedesh

BASHAN
(OG)

Misrephoth-maim

Hazor

Ashtaroth

Accho

Merom

Madon

Sea of Chinnereth

Mt. Carmel

Dor

Megiddo

Shimron

Beth-shan

Edrei

Gilead

Jordan River

Jabbok R.

Shechem
Mt. Gerizim
Mt. Ebal

Shiloh

Joppa

Aphek

Gibeon Ai

Jazer

Rabbath-ammon

AMMON

Gezer

Ashdod

Makkedah

Jericho

Gilgal

Heshbon

Libnah

Jarmuth

Jerusalem (Jebus)

Mt. Nebo (Pisgah)

Jahaz

Dibon

Ashkelon

Gath

Lachish

Bethlehem

Eglon

Debir

Hebron

Gaza (Azzah)

Beer-sheba

Hormah
Unsuccessful invasion.

Wilderness of Zin

Salt Sea (Dead)

Arnon R.

MOAB

Kir-moab

Zoar

Zered R.

Ije-abarim

Bozrah

Oboth

Punon

EDOM

MT. SEIR

Mt. Hor? (Jebel Harun)

1

THE LAND OF EGYPT

Stretching a distance of six hundred miles from Aswan (ancient Syene) at the First Cataract of the Nile, northward to the Mediterranean, is the narrow strip of cultivable land that comprised ancient Egypt.[1] The Greek historian Herodotus stated that Egypt is the gift of the Nile, for the strip of fertile land produced by the flooding of the Nile is the only break in the Sahara and Libyan deserts which stretch across North Africa to the Red Sea, and continue beyond it as the Arabian Desert. The deserts which stretch interminably to the east and west of the Nile valley made access to ancient Egypt quite difficult, and explain in part the somewhat isolated history of the country in early times.

The English name "Egypt" is derived from the Greek and Latin forms of the ancient *Ha-ku-ptah,* an earlier name for the city of Memphis, near modern Cairo. When Memphis served as capital of Egypt, its name was apparently used for the whole country, just as the city of Babylon gave its name to the Babylonian Empire. Egypt was also known to its own people as *Ta-meri,* "the beloved land," and *Kemet,* "the black country," a name descriptive of the black soil of the Nile Valley which contrasted with the nearby *Deshret,* or red country, which gives us our word "desert." The Hebrews and other Semites use the name *Misrayim,* which, in the form "Mizraim," appears in the English Bible as the second son of Ham and the Progenitor of the Ludim, Lehabim, Naphtuhim, Casluhim, and Caphtorim (Gen. 10:6, 13).

From Mount Ruwenzori, near the equator, the Nile Valley extends 2,450 air miles northward to the Mediterranean. The actual length of the Nile valley, however, including the numerous twists and turns in its tortuous route, amounts to about

---

1. *Herodotus* ii. 18.

four thousand miles, making it the second longest river valley on earth. The valley was formed as the water cut its way through sandstone and limestone, which is traversed in six places by granite and other hard stones creating cataracts which interfere with navigation and serve as natural boundaries for Nile Valley peoples. The region of the Fourth Cataract was settled by the people known in the Bible as Cushites whose kingdom became known as Cush or Ethiopia. Between the Fourth and Third Cataracts is Jebel Barkal, the southernmost point of Egyptian rule during the New Kingdom, when Cush was under an Egyptian viceroy. The land of Nubia, rich in gold, lay between the Third and First Cataracts. The remains of Abu Simbel, two huge shrines hewn out of living rock by Rameses II, are north of the Second Cataract. Their chapels, stelae, and inscriptions suggest something of the history that passed up and down the Nile.

The Nile Valley from Aswan, at the First Cataract, to the Mediterranean provided Egypt with about 13,300 square miles of cultivable land, roughly equivalent in area to Belgium or the American states of Massachusetts and Connecticut. Only the northern part of the Nile Delta lies within reach of the winter rains of the Mediterranean. Alexandria, in the western Delta, has about eight inches of rain annually, falling during the late autumn and early winter. Cairo, at the head of the Delta, has but one and one-half to two inches, mostly in January, and rain is so rare in Upper Egypt that it is looked upon as a miracle. Often years go by with no rain at all. The only fertility that comes to the land is brought by the flood waters of the Nile which deposit on its banks both moisture and rich alluvial soil washed down from central Africa.

The Egyptians were puzzled concerning the source of the Nile, flowing as it does northward from the central part of Africa. Mythology suggested that the river had its origin in heaven, and that it fell to the earth far to the south of their land. The *Book of the Dead* states that it sprang from four sources at the Twelfth Gate of the netherworld.[2] Legend also suggested that it emerged from the netherworld at the First Cataract, near modern Aswan. Even Herodotus was puzzled at conflicting views concerning the sources of the Nile. One, which he affirms is "most in error," holds that "the Nile flows from where snows melt." This is impossible, according to Herodotus,

2. Chapter 146.

for the river flows "from the hottest places to lands that are for the most part cooler." Herodotus, of course, did not know of the snow-capped mountains which actually did provide one of the sources of the Nile.[3]

The main stream, known as the White Nile, flowing from the mountainous region of central Africa provides a steady flow of water throughout the year. This is augmented by the Blue Nile, flowing from Lake Tana in the Abyssinian plateau, which becomes a mountain torrent from June to September as a result of heavy spring rains. Near Khartoum, in the Sudan, the Blue Nile joins the White Nile in its northward course. Two hundred miles farther downstream, the Atbara, the Nile's only significant tributary brings additional flood waters into the Nile from the highlands of Ethiopia. It is the water from the Blue Nile and the Atbara, added to the more steady stream of the White Nile, that bring about the annual inundation on which the economy of Egypt depends.

Although an annual flood was predictable, its extent varied from year to year. Too much water would sweep away dykes and canal banks and destroy the mud brick homes in Egyptian villages. Too little water would result in famine and starvation.

Such a famine is known to have taken place during the reign of Pharaoh Zoser, the builder of the famed Step Pyramid, who reigned about 2600 B.C. An inscription discovered near the First Cataract of the Nile, dating from about 100 B.C. says:

I was in distress on the Great Throne, and was in affliction of heart because of a very great evil, for in my time the Nile has not overflowed for a period of seven years. There was scarcely any grain; fruits were dried up; and everything which they eat was short. Every man robbed his neighbor....[4]

Zoser lived about a thousand years before Joseph, the Hebrew slave who became Prime Minister of Egypt. Joseph gained the confidence of the Pharaoh by interpreting his dreams and by suggesting a plan whereby food might be stored during the years of prosperity so that there would be ample supplies during the famine years which would follow (Gen. 41:28-57).

The annual inundation usually begins at Aswan at the end of May or the beginning of June, and the Nile continues to rise until early in September. In Memphis, at the head of the

---

3. *Herodotus* ii. 20-34 contains a full discussion of Greek and Egyptian ideas concerning the source of the Nile. The subject seems to have fascinated him.
4. A translation of the text, first published by H. K. Brugsch in 1891, appears in James A. Pritchard, ed. *Ancient Near Eastern Texts Relating to the Old Testament* (Princeton: University Press, 1955), p. 31.

Delta, the flood stage is reached from one to two weeks later. By building dams, dykes, and canals, the Egyptians were able to control the flooding, and to slow down the rate at which the waters would normally subside. Lake Moeris in the Faiyum, the predecessor of the modern Birket Qarun, was praised by classical writers as the earliest attempt to use the flood waters to provide for irrigation on a prolonged basis. Pharaohs of the Twelfth Dynasty had seen the possibilities of diverting the waters of the Nile into the Faiyum area during the inundation period.

The necessity for control of the Nile was a factor in uniting Egypt and encouraging a tendency toward centralized authority. A strong government could sponsor a program of public construction to make the best use of the Nile. During the inundation season, when agricultural work was at a standstill, the peasant's time could be utilized in building drainage canals and other public works. Herodotus says that the laborers who built the Great Pyramid worked during three month shifts. Pyramid construction probably took place during the inundation season when labor in the fields was impossible. Pyramid building did not harm the economy because the fields were neglected, but because the labor could have been expended in more productive ways. Had effort been made to develop irrigation projects rather than to build tombs for the Pharaohs, the standard of living for the entire people could have been raised significantly. This judgment is a modern one, to be sure. Those who believed that Pharaoh was a god worked on his pyramid with the same devotion that medieval Christians expended on the building of great cathedrals.

Before the beginnings of history, the small states or nomes of ancient Egypt were united into two kingdoms: Lower Egypt comprising the Delta; the Upper Egypt, the Nile Valley from Memphis at the apex of the Delta to Aswan, at the First Cataract. Even in historical times when the states were united under one Pharaoh, Egyptians spoke of their country as "The Two Lands," and the ruler bore the title, "King of Upper and Lower Egypt," and wore a double crown.

The tableland of Upper Egypt is from one to twenty-four miles in width, hugging the shores of the Nile. From his fertile valley the Egyptian could look to the east or the west and see barren desert cliffs as high as 1,800 feet. Quite naturally he regarded Egypt as the one land particularly blessed of the gods. Even the border at the First Cataract was protected by a series of cascades and rapids which served as a natural barrier to the movement of hostile peoples from the south.

The Egyptian Delta area had been a large gulf in remote prehistoric times when the area around Cairo bordered the Mediterranean. As the Nile waters made their way to the sea however, they deposited alluvium in the gulf at their mouth, and the Delta slowly emerged, becoming the Lower Egypt of historical times. As the Nile waters entered the Delta they were diverted into a number of branches, only two of which have persisted into modern times, the others having largely dried up. At its widest extent the Delta extends about 125 miles. Because of its proximity to the Mediterranean, the Delta had contacts with the outside world, and its inhabitants did not enjoy the isolation which characterized the people of Upper Egypt. The Delta was the great reservoir of land in ancient Egypt, with a dozen or so important towns, each of which was surrounded by fertile soil suitable for agriculture or the grazing of cattle. Pharaohs and their nobles enjoyed hunting in the thickets of the Delta where the jackal, fox, hyena, lion, lynx, and leopard were common. The reeds of the Delta marshes were used in making papyrus, the writing material of ancient Egypt which was the forerunner of our paper. Papyrus was also used in making baskets, sandals, small ships, and rope.

Bordering Egypt to the northeast was the Sinai Peninsula, an arid region which served as a buffer zone between Egypt and the nations of Asia. The civilized Egyptians built a wall on their border and sought to keep from their land the nomadic people of the desert, but in times of Egyptian weakness the bedouin were able to enter and settle down. Through the centuries Egypt was invaded by a succession of Hyksos, Assyrians, Babylonians, Persians, and Arabs who crossed the Sinai Peninsula and occupied Egypt. Conversely, during Egypt's Empire Period, she penetrated western Asia as far as the upper reaches of the Euphrates. Nevertheless the Sinai Peninsula discouraged such contacts, and military ventures often had to be supplemented by naval control of the eastern Mediterranean.

Early man lived on the desert plateau which today stretches along both sides of the Nile Valley. Although the Libyan and the Sahara deserts are now barren except for a few oases, there was a time when they received enough rain to make possible life on a relatively large scale. In regions that are now completely barren, strata reveal the presence of hippopotami, buffalo, wild asses, gazelles, and ostriches. At the end of this period African climate changed markedly, for the rain belt shifted, the wells began to dry up, and man and beast had to retreat to regions which afforded a means of livelihood. As bordering lands became desert, the Nile Valley continued to provide fertile ground.

People of differing races moved into the Nile Valley long before the dawn of history. The earliest inhabitants appear to have been a hunting people of the "Brown Mediterranean" type. Their tombs have yielded hunting knives, and the remains of dogs which were domesticated and trained as companions on the chase. After settling in the Nile Valley, the earliest Egyptians domesticated cattle, and subsequently became cultivators of the soil.

Early in historic times the basic Mediterranean population of Egypt was modified by groups of Asiatics of Anatolian and Semitic descent who settled from time to time on the eastern frontier of the Delta. They are known to have been in Egypt at the end of the Sixth Dynasty (ca. 2250 B.C.), and the Asiatic Hyksos actually ruled Egypt from about 1720 to 1550 B.C. During the time of Joseph, a Semitic Israelite who became Prime Minister of Egypt, the Israelite tribes settled in the district of the western Delta known as Goshen (Gen. 46).

Characteristically, the ancient Egyptian was tall and thin. He had reddish brown skin and long, curly black hair. Usually he wore a short beard. He had full lips, a long skull, and almond-shaped eyes. His hands were quite small. The ancient Egyptians spoke a Hamito-Semitic language which has been preserved in writing since about 3000 B.C. Its latest form, Coptic, is still used as a liturgical language in the Coptic Church. The Egyptian language seems to have been built on a Hamitic, African base to which numerous Semitic elements were added. These include a considerable amount of vocabulary, as well as prefixes, suffixes, and verb forms. The Egyptian verb, like that of the Semitic languages, is based on a tri-consonantal root.

The alluvium which provided Egypt with excellent soil made it inevitable that her economy would be based on agriculture. Egyptians lived in small villages, which they left each morning to tend their farms. Although theoretically all land belonged to the king, in practice the Egyptians treated their soil, cattle, and homes as private property, paying the required taxes to the government. Barley was the principal agricultural crop, with wheat and emmer occupying a secondary position. Egyptian flax made possible the manufacture of a high grade of linen, for which Egypt became famous. Fruits and melons were also grown in considerable quantity. Although the Egyptian became a food-producer before historic times, the abundance of life in the Nile made it inevitable that he would not abandon hunting entirely. Fish, geese, and ducks supplemented the food grown by Egyptian peasants on their small farms.

The Bible mentions the antipathy felt by the Egyptians of the Nile Valley toward the bedouin who tended flocks of sheep and goats (Gen. 46:34). Not only did Israel settle in the land of Goshen, east of the Delta, but bedouin have kept their flocks in that general area throughout history. Even today, Arab bedouin regularly appear in the Wadi Tumilat area between Lake Timsah and the Delta. The pasture land is covered with clumps of bulrushes, papyrus, and shrubs.

While the Egyptian frowned upon the nomadic bedouin with his sheep and goats, large cattle were raised in Egypt itself, and they were so abundant that their hides became an export commodity. The Hyksos invaders introduced the horse into Egypt (*ca.* 1700 B.C.), and in subsequent years Egypt was noted for its fine horses (cf. I Kings 10:28-29). The donkey was the caravan animal of ancient nomads who entered Egypt, as we know from the Beni Hasan tomb painting which depicts Semitic traders with their retinue. The camel was rare in Egypt until Persian times.

Semites entering Egypt. The Israelites who entered Egypt during the days of Joseph may have looked like these Semites of the nineteenth century B.C. depicted in a tomb at Beni Hasan.

Courtesy, Oriental Institute, University of Chicago

Egypt had a decided advantage over Mesopotamia in her natural supply of stone from nearby cliffs. Whereas Sumer and Babylon built their temples and palaces of mud brick, Egypt could use limestone, alabaster, granite, and basalt in her major buildings. Copper was available from the mines of Sinai, and Nubia was a ready source of gold, which was also mined in the hills between the Nile and the Red Sea. Egypt did not have a native supply of iron, however. With the beginnings of the Iron Age she was at a disadvantage because all her iron had to be imported. Egypt was also poor in wood. Her papyrus and shrubs could serve some minor needs, but good wood had to be imported from Phoenicia. Early in her history, Egypt maintained trade relations with Byblos (ancient Gebel) on the Syrian coast where she secured the famed cedar trees of Lebanon, along with fir and cyprus trees.

The history of Egypt is traditionally divided into thirty dynasties, extending from the time when Upper and Lower Egypt were unified under Menes (ca. 2980 B.C.) to Alexander's conquest (332 B.C.) The first two dynasties, which ruled from This, or Thinis, are known as the Early Dynastic or Thinite Period. Dynasties three to eight (ca. 2676-2194 B.C.) comprise the Old Kingdom, or Pyramid Age, when Pharoahs reigned from Memphis with unchallenged control. The absolutism of the Old Kingdom ended in a time of social upheaval known as the First Intermediate Period (ca. 2160-1991 B.C.) during which local princes gained power at the expense of the central government. Their rule covers Dynasties nine through eleven. The establishment of the powerful Twelfth Dynasty at Thebes (ca. 1991 B.C.) ushered in the brilliant Middle Kingdom (ca. 1991-1670 B.C.) during which literature and the arts flourished.

Egypt experienced her most trying hour during the Second Intermediate Period (ca. 1670-1568 B.C.), comprising Dynasties fifteen and sixteen, when Asiatic Hyksos seized control and reigned from Avaris in the eastern Delta. Kings of the Seventeenth Dynasty began the liberation of Egypt, and Ahmose, founder of the Eighteenth Dynasty, expelled the Hyksos and ushered in Egypt's New Kingdom, or Empire Period (1568-1085 B.C.) Egyptian armies marched into western Asia and controlled territory as far north as the Euphrates River. Dynasties nineteen and twenty mark the Rameside age, at the end of which a period of decline began from which Egypt never fully recovered. Dynasties twenty-one to twenty-three (1085-718 B.C.) were a period of transition, during which Israel became a monarchy under Saul and David. Solomon married an Egyptian princess, but relations with Egypt subsequently deteriorated, and Jeroboam was able to find a place of asylum there, from which he returned to challenge Rehoboam's right to the throne. Egypt sought to control Palestine through invasions and alliances designed to hold in check the rival Assyrian Empire in the East.

Dynasties twenty-five and twenty-six comprise the Late Period (750-525 B.C.) during which Ethiopian kings from Napata struggled with Assyrians for lordship over Egypt, and Saite kings including Necho and Apries (Hophra) fought on Palestinian battlefields and promised aid to the states of western Asia that would resist Assyria and Babylonia. Dynasties twenty-seven to thirty comprise the Persian Period (525-341 B.C.) following the conquest of Egypt by Cambyses. Egypt tried to throw off the Persian yoke, and was periodically successful until 332 B.C. when Alexander the Great conquered Egypt, whose people looked upon him as a deliverer, and the Hellenistic Age began.

2

EGYPTIAN RELIGION

In the earliest days each village in Egypt looked to its own deity for the blessings of life and protection against hostile powers, human or demonic. The village would boast a shrine to its deity, and the worship of the local god served as a unifying influence within the community and a means of distinguishing one village from another.

Many of the names of these early village gods have been preserved in later traditions. Ptah was the god of Memphis, Atum of nearby Heliopolis. Ancient Thebes was dedicated to the worship of Montu. Khnum had his shrine at Herwer, near the First Cataract, and Min was worshiped at Coptos. Sometimes the god had no name distinct from the village in which he was worshiped. The god of Ombos is simply known as "the Ombite," and "He of Edfu" describes the god of that community.

Goddesses as well as gods claimed the allegiance of the Nile Valley peoples. Hathor was the "Lady of Dendera," and Neith was the goddess of Sais. Her name appears in Asenath (literally "She is of Neith"), the daughter of Potiphera, priest at On (Heliopolis), who married Joseph and was the mother of Ephraim and Manasseh (Gen. 41:45, 50-52; 46:20). The protective goddess of Memphis was Sekhmet, and Sobek was goddess in the Faiyum.

As the small Egyptian communities united to become states, or nomes, local gods gained a wider recognition; and when the two empires of Upper Egypt (the Nile Valley) and Lower Egypt (the Delta) came into being, two of the local gods — Seth of Ombos and Horus of Behdet — became the gods of the two nations. The political situation was explained in terms of a struggle for supremacy among the gods, each of whom took as his share half of Egypt.

About 3000 B.C., when Egypt became a unified state under

Nar-mer (Menes), Upper Egypt emerged as the dominant part of the country and Horus became god of "the two Egypts" — as the combined empire of Upper and Lower Egypt was called. The Pharaoh was considered the incarnation and patron of Horus and was therefore considered a god in his own right.

During the three thousand years of ancient Egyptian history the gods gained and lost popularity and religion itself acquired many nuances which would have been strange to the earliest Egyptians. The vulture goddess of Nekheb (Elkab) and the serpent goddess of Buto became national deities during one of the periods when north and south were divided. The worship of Amon was transferred from Hermopolis to Thebes during the Eleventh Dynasty. Later, Amon was identified with Re and the national god of the New Kingdom became "Amon-Re, King of the Gods."

As people moved from place to place they brought their local gods with them and erected new shrines for their worship. On occasion the god of a particular community gained a reputation for special power as the result of some supposedly potent cure or display of miraculous intervention. As a result, people from neighboring areas would make pilgrimages to the god's shrine, or build him new shrines in their own villages. In some such way, Neith of Sais acquired a shrine at Esna.

At an early date local deities came to be associated with some distinctive characteristic, so that the falcon-shaped Montu was worshiped as a war god and Min of Coptos became a god of fertility and harvest, and patron of desert travelers. Ptah of Memphis, in whose province the distinctive art of Egypt originated, became patron of artists, smiths, and metal workers. As such he may be compared with the Canaanite Kathar-wa-Khassis, the classical Hephaestus, and the Teutonic Vulcan.

Sekhmet of Memphis was a fire goddess who annihilated her enemies, while the more kindly Hathor of Dendera was a goddess of love and joy. The falcon god Horus, identified with the sun, was pictured as a youthful hero in perpetual battle with his evil brother Seth, the storm god. The ibis-headed Thoth, of Hermopolis, was the moon god who had created the divisions of time and order in the universe. Thoth was "lord of divine words," who had invented hieroglyphic writing and was the god of learning in general. Sobek, the crocodile god, had his home in the water.

In addition to the numerous city gods, an ancient Egyptian was concerned with a multitude of lesser gods, demons, and spirits who might either help or injure man. There were gods who assisted women in childbirth, gods of the household, and gods of the harvest. In times of illness, spirits provided healing, and others were particularly active in time of war. Ma^{c}at was the goddess of truth and justice.

When the people of a district lived in peace and enjoyed fellowship with one another, the local gods shared in this fellowship. Gods might actually be taken to a neighboring city to pay a visit to that city's deity. An outside god might be presented with his own chapel in the temple of the city god, so that eventually the god of a powerful and wealthy city might be surrounded by the images of gods and demigods.

In time certain gods came to be grouped together as family units. In the temple of Karnak at Thebes we meet the god Amon, the goddess Mut, and their son Khonsu (the moon). Similarly at Memphis we find Ptah, Sekhmet and Nefertem. At Abydos we meet the favored family of Osiris, Isis, and Horus.

The outward manifestations of the gods of Egypt were crude, and historians wonder how a people so advanced in many areas of culture could be so crass in matters of religious devotion. Neith was represented as a shield to which a pair of crossed arrows had been nailed, and Busiris was depicted in the form of a pillar with the head and arms of a king. Ptah of Memphis and Min of Coptos were fetishes in semi-human form.

Most common were the representations of deities in animal form. Sobek, the crocodile; Thoth, the ibis; Khnum, the ram; Hathor, the cow; and Buto, the serpent are but a few of the gods depicted as animals.

It was customary to have the wooden statue of a god in its own shrine in the local temple. On feast days the statue would be removed and carried in procession on the shoulders of priests, or transported on the river in a sacred bark. When a particular animal was sacred to a given temple, specimens of that animal were kept in the Temple. Strabo, in the time of Augustus Caesar, mentions the crocodile sacred to Sobek at Arsinoe, capital of the Faiyum:

> It is fed with the bread, meat, and wine brought by the strangers who come to see it. Our host went with us to the lake, taking along a small meal-cake, some meat, and a small flask of wine. We found the animal lying on the bank; the priests approached, and while some of them opened his jaws, another thrust first the cake into his mouth, then the meat, and finally poured the wine after them. Thereupon the crocodile plunged into the lake and swam to the opposite shore.

From very ancient times the Egyptians represented their gods in human forms as well. Gods appeared with human face and

(Left) Stele of Rameses II. Below the sun disk, Rameses II (right) stands before his god Amon-Re. Between the two figures are vessels, probably captured by Rameses and offered to his god. The lower part of the stele lists the names of conquered foes.

Courtesy, University Museum, Philadelphia

(Below) Rameses II displays his prowess. A cylinder seal from Bethshan depicts Rameses shooting at a target supported by a pole. His Syrian foes are tied back to back. To the right of Rameses is a god (possibly Seth) with a scimitar in his left hand and the ankh ("life") sign in his right hand.

Courtesy, University Museum, Philadelphia

figure, wearing the same clothing as the Egyptians. Their head
was adorned with a helmet or crown. In their hands were a
baton and a scepter, symbolic of authority. The goddess would
carry a papyrus blossom with a long stem.

Gods which had been depicted in animal form were transferred into human figures surmounted by the heads of the
sacred animals. Thus Sobek might be depicted as a crocodile, or
as a man with the head of a crocodile. Khnum became a man
with a ram's head; Horus a man with the head of a falcon;
Thoth a man with the head of an ibis. The goddess Sekhmet
became a woman with the head of a lionness.

In addition to local deities identified with animals, Egypt had
several sacred animals which were particularly venerated. Most
important was the Apis Bull of Memphis which, according to a
legend preserved in Greek sources, was begotten by a ray of
sunlight which descended from heaven and impregnated a cow.
The Apis Bull was black, with white spots including a white
triangle on the forehead and the figure of a crescent moon on the
right side. Usually he wore a red cloth on his back. As early as
the Old Kingdom, priests were assigned to care for the Apis
Bull. Later theological speculation sought to discover a relationship between the Bull and Ptah, the god of Memphis. As a result the Apis Bull was declared to be the son of Ptah, or "the
living reincarnation of Ptah."

During New Kingdom times deceased bulls were given elaborate burials in mausoleums at Saqqara near Memphis. Rameses
II laid out an elaborate gallery in which bulls were buried in
stone sarcophagi. The gallery, known as the Serapeum was
carved out of solid rock. It was three hundred fifty feet long
with rows of niches for the burial of individual bulls. Many
pious pilgrims came to the Serapeum to venerate the bulls as
late as the Ptolemaic period.

In addition to the divine Pharaoh, certain other humans
were deified by the Egyptians and accorded a place in the
pantheon. The famous architect Imhotep who served as chief
minister to Pharaoh Zoser was regarded as the son of Ptah and
became an Egyptian god of wisdom and medicine. Imhotep's
greatest accomplishment was the Step Pyramid which he designed for Zoser at Saqqarah, near Memphis. His fame was
known to the Greeks who called him Imouthes and identified
him with their god of healing, Asklepios. Divinity was also
ascribed to Amenophis, son of Hapu, the minister of the Eighteenth Dynasty Pharaoh Amenhotep III.

The phenomena of nature — sun, moon, stars, heaven, earth, the Nile — all had a place in Egyptian religion. The sky god was pictured as a falcon with protective wings spread over Egypt, or over all the earth. The sun and moon were his divine eyes, and the stars were attached to his body. Wind is the breadth of his mouth, and water his perspiration.

In another nature myth the sky was depicted as the goddess Nut. In primordial times she was embraced by the earth god, Geb, until Shu — god of the atmosphere — separated them by elevating Nut high above the earth and placing himself beneath her. From the union of Geb and Nut — earth and heaven — there sprang a son, Re, the sun god and the most popular of all the cosmic gods. He travels by day in his bark across the celestial ocean. When night comes he transfers to another boat, descends to the netherworld and continues his voyage.

Re also was depicted as a falcon soaring through the sky with bright plumage, or as a young hero carrying on a constant struggle with the hostile powers of darkness. As the god of Edfu in Upper Egypt, Re often appears as a sun disk with extended wings, the form in which he regularly appears as a symbol of protection over doors and elsewhere in Egyptian temples. It became customary for Egyptians to present offerings to Re under the open sky. Pharoahs of the Fifth Dynasty considered themselves the children of Re. He had a temple near Memphis which had, as its chief feature, an obelisk erected on a stone substructure.

In the development of Egyptian theology, connections were seen between the local gods and celestial powers. The falcon shaped Horus was identified with the sky god and became Harakhti, "Horus of the Horizon." He in turn was identified with Re, giving the doubly compound name Re-Harakhti, "Re-Horus of the Horizon." In this form Re appears as a king with the head of a falcon surmounted by the sun disk, from which hangs the uraeus serpent, a symbol of royalty.

The crocodile, Sobek, and the ram, Khnum, along with Amon of Thebes were identified with Re and assigned the sun disk and uraeus as signs of rank. Local gods retained their old attributes and myths alongside the newer identifications so that the religion contained many confusing and self-contradicting ideas. There were efforts to distinguish various phases of the sun god, so that Khepri, the sun in the form of a scarab, was worshiped as the morning sun, and Atum as the evening sun.

The female deities tended to become identified with the sky

goddess Nut. When Hathor, the cow goddess was identified with Nut, mythology suggested that the sky was an enormous cow, held fast by numerous gods and supported in position by Shu, god of the atmosphere. The stars were attached to the cow's belly and the sun-god travelled in his bark around her body.

The cat goddess of Bubastis, and the lionesses Sekhmet and Pekhet were identified with Mut, the consort of Amon and mother of the gods. Hathor and Isis were also identified. Amon of Karnak, Min of Coptos, and Khnum of Elephantine were combined into a single deity.

While the confusion produced by the Egyptian religious concepts may seem to defy schematization, the priests at the religious centers did try to work out logical theologies. The best known formulation dates from Fifth Dynasty Heliopolis. Here the priests described the self-engendered Atum emerging from primeval chaos, bringing the cosmos into being. From himself, Atum produced Shu, the god of the air, and Tefnut, goddess of moisture. The union of this couple produced Geb, the earth god, and Nut, the sky goddess. They, in turn, produced four children: Osiris who represented the forces of life, and his wife-sister Isis; Seth, representing the force of destruction, and his wife-sister Nephthys. The nine gods and goddesses: Shu, Tefnut, Geb, Osiris, Isis, Seth, and Nephthys are known as the Ennead.

The priests at Hermopolis taught that eight primordial gods were created from primeval chaos by the voice of Thoth. Four frogs represent the male deities, with four snakes representing the female principle. These deities produced at Hermopolis an egg from which emerged the sun who conquered his enemies created mankind, and organized the world as we know it.

As early as Old Kingdom times a theology was developed at Memphis which exalted the god Ptah as chief of the pantheon. Ptah made eight other Ptahs, all embodied in himself. Atum was the thought of Ptah, Horus, his heart, and Thoth his tongue.

By historical times the Egyptian local gods, cosmic deities, and gods responsible for some function or aspect of life were so blended that one name bore numerous connotations. Thoth was god of Hermopolis, but he was also the moon god and the god of wisdom. Hathor was goddess of Dendera, a sky goddess, and goddess of love.

Once during the history of Pharaonic Egypt the established religion was challenged by a reformer. The Eighteenth dynasty Pharaoh Amenhotep IV devoted himself to the god Aton, one

of the manifestations of the sun god of Heliopolis. After breaking with the Amon priesthood at Thebes, the capital of New
Kingdom Egypt, Amenhotep IV took to himself the name Akhenaton and moved his capital to Akhetaton, modern Tell
el-Amarna, where he encouraged new concepts of literature and
art as well as the new religious emphasis. Akhenaton banned all
religious activity except that which was addressed to Aton, and
as a result is frequently considered a monotheist. His was not,
however, the spiritual monotheism which was represented by
Israel's prophets, but rather a monotheism which exalted the
disk of the sun to a pre-eminent position. Akhenaton's reforms
did not long outlive their chief exponent, and the priests of
Amon were able to reassert the religious philosophy of the
old regime during the lifetime of Tutankhamon, Akhenaton's
son-in-law.

In Old Kingdom times the Pharaoh was theoretically the
sole priest, but in practice he delegated authority to the nom-

Tutankhamon and his god. A black granite statue depicts the god Amon (large
figure) with Pharaoh Tutankhamon, who
renounced the Aton faith of Akhenaton
and returned to Thebes, the center of the
Amon priesthood.   Courtesy, The Louvre

archs and other officials for the performance of the religious rites. It was during the Middle Kingdom that the professional priesthood evolved, and by New Kingdom times the priesthood had developed to the point where four companies of priests served in rotation, a month at a time. Priests were permitted to marry and they engaged in commerce, trade, and other secular activities when not officiating in the temples.

The afterlife was uppermost in Egyptian thought, and much of the energy expended by the inhabitants of the Nile Valley had as its goal the provision for a happy future. Egyptian religion taught that man could live on in the future exactly as he had lived on earth provided the necessities for such existence were available. Tombs were provided with jars of food and drink. Wealthy Egyptians or their relatives established endowments, the income from which was to furnish food for the deceased for all time. Children were expected to provide for their parents' welfare in the next life. Walls of tombs were covered with representations of food, drink, and other objects which might serve the deceased, and it was thought that these pictures might magically be transformed into the actual objects.

The deceased also depended upon the prayers of survivors to guarantee their welfare. Visitors who chanced to pass a tomb were invited to repeat prayers which could magically conjure up all that was needed for the nourishment and enjoyment of the deceased. Food, drink, oils, ointments, cosmetics — all that might be useful to the departed in the next life — could be made available by the faithful prayers of relatives and friends.

The lavish furnishings of the tombs of Egyptian Pharaohs can best be imagined by viewing the articles discovered by Howard Carter in the tomb of Tutankhamon in the Valley of the Kings, west of Luxor, ancient Thebes. Tutankhamon was a minor Pharaoh who died young, but the wealth of objects discovered in his tomb staggers the imagination. They are the most treasured exhibits in the Cairo Museum today.

The Egyptian thought of man as a creature with a body and a soul (Egyptian *Ba*) which was pictured as a bird which departs the body at death and flies around the world. At night the *ba* might return to the safety of the tomb, but this could take place only if the body of the deceased was properly preserved. To prevent decomposition and enable the soul to recognize the body the Egyptians developed the art of mummification. The *ba* could, by means of magical formulas, transform itself into a falcon, a serpent, a lily, or a crocodile. The Greeks erroneously interpreted this as a doctrine of the transmigration of the soul.

In addition to the *Ba*, the Egyptian also had a *Ka*, a protective spirit or genius who was born simultaneously with the individual and had a close relation to him throughout life. The *Ka* did not die with the individual, but survived the deceased to quicken him with life and strength and protect him from his enemies in the next life.

Domestic gods were also concerned with the well being of departed ones in the grave. Many cities had special mortuary gods, including Khenty-Imentiu, "The first of the westerners" (i.e., the dead) who was represented as a jackall. Such deities early receded in favor of Osiris, the deified king of Busiris who met a tragic death by drowning in the Nile. While Abydos became the chief center for the worship of Osiris, his fame spread throughout Egypt. The saga of his life and death was the most appealing of all the stories of Egypt's gods. Although it has not been preserved in Egyptian texts, it is known from the writings of Plutarch.

Osiris was a good king, but Seth, his wicked brother, had designs on the throne. Seth, by trickery, had his brother lay himself in an artistically wrought chest, whereupon seventy-two henchmen of the usurper sprang upon the chest, closed the lid, and cast it into the Nile River. It was carried by the waters of the Nile to the Mediterranean, then along the Palestinian coast as far as Byblos where it landed. In the meantime Isis, the lovely sister and wife of Osiris journeyed throughout the world seeking the body of her husband. After finding it at Byblos, she carried it back to Egypt and mourned for her departed loved one.

Since the wicked Seth was now on the throne of Egypt, Isis had to act with utmost caution. She concealed the coffin and went to Buto, in the Delta marshes, to stay with her son Horus. While on a hunting expedition, Seth came upon the coffin of his hated brother. He divided the body into fourteen pieces and scattered them throughout Egypt. Isis, however, learned of this insult to her dead husband and again went in search of his remains. She discovered them and erected a monument over each. When the lad Horus grew to manhood he avenged the death of his father by winning a victory over Seth. Through the magic of Horus, Osiris was brought back to life and ruled in the west as king of the blessed dead.

By identification with Osiris, the Egyptians hoped to share

in his victory and immortality. As Osiris had died, so they knew they must die, but because Osiris had been given life again, so they hoped for a blessed future. The faithfulness of Horus in using the proper formulas to bring his father back to life suggested that faithful sons of all Egyptians might perform the proper rites to insure to their parents a blessed future. In this way the deceased might actually become Osiris.

The entrance into the blessed realm of Osiris depended on the proper use of magical formulas and spells, but they were valueless unless the deceased had lived a virtuous life on earth. At death each individual appeared for judgment in the presence of Osiris who sat with a court of forty-two judges. The deceased sought to convince his judges that he had been innocent of wrong-doing throughout life. After he had given his defense his heart was weighed in the balances before the god Thoth. If his heart was found to be guiltless, the individual entered a blessed future life.

The dwelling place of the dead was in the west — the region of the sunset. The departed might be transferred into shining stars in the heavens or, in mundane fashion, as living in celestial fields of rushes where they cultivated soil, plowed, sowed, and reaped as on earth. There, however, grain grew seven cubits (twelve feet) high — a wonderful paradise for the Egyptian peasant!

Labor, however, did not seem desirable in a heavenly paradise, and after the Middle Kingdom we find mummiform figures placed in the tombs of the deceased. They are provided with farm implements and sacred symbols to perform the menial tasks of the future life. These figurines, known as *Ushabtiu,* bore the names of the deceased whom they were to serve. Magical formulas inscribed on the figures could bring them to life and enable them to perform their duties.

The Egyptian "Book of What is in the Netherworld" describes an earth beneath the world of the living, with a stream — a subterranean Nile — flowing through its length. This earth is divided into twelve parts, corresponding to the twelve hours of the night. The parts are separated from each other by great gates. The ram-headed sun god, surrounded by a royal retinue, sails his bark on the stream bringing light and life for a time to those who inhabit the nether regions. The nightly voyages bring joy to the deceased, who become for a time companions of the sun god. At dawn, however, the sun god leaves the subterranean world to enter the upper world and journey across the celestial ocean where the living may behold him.

Earliest Egyptian burials were simple affairs. The body was placed on its left side in a natural sleeping position. Knees were against the body and hands before the face. In Old Kingdom times, the period of the earliest Pharaohs, bodies were stretched out full length and placed in tombs. Mummification was practiced to prevent deterioration of the body. The viscera were removed and the resulting cavity filled with wads of linen cloth. The corpse was saturated with natron and bound with linen wrappings. Cedar oil was used at a later time. Resinous pastes were used to preserve the contour of the body.

The viscera were interred in four vases, protected by four deities responsible for guaranteeing the deceased against hunger and thirst. In rich burials, the vases were placed in chests constructed in the form of a chapel adorned with representations of the gods and religious inscriptions. The process of mummification lasted seventy days, after which the body was laid in its coffin and removed to the tomb. In Old Kingdom times the coffin was a rectangular chest of stone or wood. It was made in the form of a house with doors to symbolize the concept that the coffin was a house for the dead. During the Eighteenth Dynasty the coffin was in the form of a man or woman arrayed in the costume of the time, or in the form of a mummy decorated with religious pictures and inscriptions.

The Egyptian concern with the material aspects of survival — the great concern for proper mummification and the correct magical formulas — has caused many modern students to conclude that their religion was devoid of an element of personal warmth and devotion. It is true that we have little evidence of the personal side of Egyptian religion, but it does appear that Egyptians felt that their gods were near to them and were interested in their welfare. Such names as Meri-Re, "Beloved of Re," and Ptah-em-saf, "Ptah is his protection" show that religion was more than a formality to the devout.

The events preceding the Exodus may be looked upon as a contest between Yahweh, Israel's God, and the numerous gods of Egypt. The element of power is uppermost in the contest: Egypt's gods are powerless, but Yahweh is omnipotent. While Yahweh is specifically the God of Israel, He is concerned that his power be known among the Egyptians: "And the Egyptians shall know that I am Yahweh, when I stretch forth my hand upon Egypt and bring out the people of Israel from among them" (Exod. 7:5). When the Nile became putrid, and the sun (Re) was darkened, the Egyptians could see the impotence of their gods. Centuries later the Greeks and Romans expressed contempt and scorn at finding primitive religious ideas in a race so admirable for its achievements. It is one of the ironies of history that Israel, never a world power and usually a pawn between the larger states, should have been the nation through which the knowledge of the true God came while Egypt, at one time the major power in the East, never matured in religious thinking but worshiped a multitude of gods and entertained crass theories of the universe until the Jew, the Christian, and ultimately the Moslem put the death blow to the religious concepts of ancient Egypt.

Temple of Rameses II at Abu Simbel. Among the many monuments built by Rameses II is the gigantic cliff temple of Abu Simbel in Nubia. The colossal head of the Pharaoh is viewed from the south end of the facade.
Courtesy, Oriental Institute, University of Chicago

3

A PHARAOH WHO KNEW NOT JOSEPH

Joseph the Prime Minister! The recollection of the wisdom of this Semitic official who had saved Egypt from the horrors of famine must have lasted long in the memories of his grateful subjects. Yet we do not meet the name of Joseph in any Egyptian record. Ever since scholars began to decipher the hieroglyphic writing of Egypt people have wondered about the strange absence of any mention of Joseph, or Moses, or any phase of the Israelite sojourn in Egypt. Not until the reign of Merneptah (*ca.* 1224-1216 B.C.) do we meet the name of Israel, and then it appears on a stele which boasts of Egyptian victories in Canaan. Nationalistic Egyptians may have chosen to

Merneptah's Hymn of Victory. The so-called "Israel Stela" contains the line "Israel is laid waste, his seed is not." The Egyptian Pharaoh Merneptah claims to have destroyed the Israelite people during the fifth year of his reign (ca. 1230 B.C.) when he campaigned in Canaan. This is the first mention of Israel in Egyptian records. It shows that Israelites were in Canaan by the thirteenth century B.C.

Courtesy, The Cairo Museum

forget the Semite who had saved their land from the consequences of famine.

For centuries, Semites had brought their wares to Egypt and
caravans of semi-nomadic peoples bringing articles for trade
became commonplace. The nineteenth century B.C. tomb painting from Beni-Hasan depicts a group of Asiatics entering Egypt
with their families to trade eye paint for the products of the
Nile Valley.

Many Semitic traders eventually found a home in Egypt,
particularly in the eastern Delta, the region closest to Syria and
Palestine. It was in this area that Joseph encouraged his family
to settle when famine conditions had driven them out of
Canaan. Scripture calls this district the land of Goshen (Gen.
47:6, 27). Although we are not certain of the exact location of
Goshen, it is sometimes called "the land of Rameses" (cf. Gen.
47:6, 11), suggesting that it was the region adjacent to the city
of Raamses in the northeastern Delta.

The Egyptians, always proud of the culture which they had
developed in the Nile Valley and Delta, were humiliated during the years which followed the decline of the Middle Kingdom (ca. 1991-1786 B.C.). During a time of Egyptian weakness
a people known as the Hyksos seized control of the government
and ruled much of Egypt. Many of the Hyksos were Semites,
but some were Hittites and Hurrians. Manetho, a priest at
Heliopolis during the third century B.C., who wrote a history
of Egypt, said of the Hyksos:

> In his reign (i.e., Tutimaeus), for what cause I know not, a blast of
> God smote us; and unexpectedly, from the regions of the East, invaders
> of obscure race marched in confidence of victory against our land. By
> main force they easily seized it without striking a blow; and having
> overpowered the rulers of the land, they then burned our cities ruth-
> lessly, razed to the ground the temples of the gods, and treated all the
> natives with cruel hostility. . . . Finally, they appointed as king one of
> their number whose name was Salitis.[1]

Manetho is giving, to be sure, a biased picture of the Hyksos
whose rule was resented by the native Egyptians. The Hyksos
invasion probably began with the infiltration of semi-nomadic
Asiatics into the eastern Delta. During times when Egypt was
not strong enough to defend her frontiers, the Semitic peoples
from the east moved toward the lush terrain of the Nile Delta.
After establishing a hegemony over the eastern fringes of the
Delta, making Avaris their capital, the Hyksos gradually extended their power until the entire Delta, and finally Upper
Egypt as well, was subject to their power.

---

1. Quoted in Josephus, *Against Apion* I, 14.

The name Hyksos means "rulers of foreign lands," and in Manetho's list of Egyptian rulers they comprise the Fifteenth and Sixteenth Dynasties. Hyksos rule was well established by 1700 B.C. and continued for about a century and a half. Biblical scholars usually suggest that Joseph and his brothers entered Egypt during Hyksos times on the assumption that the non-Egyptian Hyksos rulers would be more likely than native born Pharaohs to promote a Semite such as Joseph to a position of authority. It is possible that the Pharaoh under whom Joseph ruled was a native Egyptian, however, for prejudices against Semites are mentioned in the Biblical text. We read that "the Egyptians might not eat bread with the Hebrews, for that is an abomination to the Egyptians" (Gen. 43:32) and that the Israelites settled in Goshen instead of the Nile valley because "every shepherd is an abomination to the Egyptians" (Gen. 46:34). Since we have no means of giving positive dates to the descent of Joseph and his family into Egypt, we cannot be certain concerning the dynasty in power when they settled in Goshen. Biblical evidence, however, suggests that Joseph's family settled in an area near Pharaoh's court (Gen. 46:28f.), a fact that argues for Hyksos times when the Empire was ruled from Avaris in the Delta.

If Joseph was given his favored position under a native dynasty, it must have been prior to the Hyksos rule. Following the period of Hyksos control, Egyptian life could never be the same. A new nationalism supplanted the older tolerance for foreigners. Egypt determined to rule rather than be ruled. Native rulers of the Eighteenth Dynasty tried to cut out of the monuments every reference to the despised Hyksos, but modern Egyptologists have been able to piece together evidence that their rule was not entirely bad. The Hyksos Empire included both Egypt and Palestine. Trade connections were maintained with Mesopotamia and the island of Crete as we know from inscriptions bearing the name of Khayan, their most famous king.

The horse and chariot were introduced into Egypt by the Hyksos invaders. The particular type of fortification used by the Hyksos has been found in Palestine and Syria as well as Egypt. Huge earth ramparts were built to enclose fortified areas for the housing of chariots. Excavations at Jericho and Shechem have brought to light such fortifications, suggesting that kings of the Palestinian city states owed feudal allegiance to the Hyksos king.

The family of Jacob-Israel that migrated to Egypt during the time of Joseph comprised about seventy people. As the population grew, Israelites probably moved out of Goshen and lived in closer proximity to their Egyptian neighbors. It is also possible that some migrated from time to time back to Canaan, their ancestral homeland. When Jacob died, Joseph and his brothers led a large retinue back to the family burial place at Hebron (Gen. 50:7-14). Through the intervening years there must have been many such caravans traversing the familiar roads eastward from Goshen.[2]

When the Israelites entered Canaan under Joshua they seem to have found some closely related peoples who recognized them as friends. Although neither the books of Joshua nor Judges state this in so many words, there is much circumstantial evidence to show that it was so. Shechem, near the boundary between Ephraim and Manasseh (Josh. 17:6), had been associated with Israelite tradition since Abraham had first entered Canaan (Gen. 12:6-7). During the fifteenth century B.C. the *Hapiru* people mentioned in the Amarna Letters occupied the city.[3] The account of the conquest of Canaan by the Israelites includes no record of battles at Shechem, but following the conquest Joshua called all of the tribes to assemble there for renewal of the covenant (Josh. 24:1-28). The people of Shechem were evidently Israelites who were in Canaan prior to the Exodus.

Although Lower and Middle Egypt seem to have become reconciled to Hyksos rule, Thebes in Upper Egypt plotted the revolt which ultimately brought native Egyptians back into power. After several generations of strife, an Egyptian named Ahmose succeeded in capturing the Hyksos capital at Avaris, in the eastern Delta, and driving them out of the country. Ahmose, according to the reckoning of Manetho, was the founder of the Eighteenth Dynasty which ushered in Egypt's New Kingdom or Empire Period. After driving them out of Egypt, Ahmose pursued the Hyksos to their stronghold at Sheruhen in southern Palestine, and spent the next six years trying to dislodge them. The years of Hyksos rule taught the Egyptians that they could not be satisfied with the isolated seclusion

---

2. W. F. Albright, BASOR 58 (April 1935), pp. 10-18 and BASOR 74 (April 1939), pp. 11-23 maintains that the Joseph tribes (Ephraim and Manasseh) were in Palestine around 1400 B.C.
3. Cf. J. B. Pritchard, ed. *Ancient Near Eastern Texts,* pp. 477, 485-87, 489, 490.

which the Nile Valley provided. The path of safety seemed to be in Empire, and Egypt sought to drive the Hyksos rulers from Palestine and rule in her own right.

The "new king over Egypt who did not know Joseph" (Exod. 1:8) must have been one of the New Kingdom rulers who did not trust foreigners in his land. The Egyptians foresaw a time when their own land would be invaded, and they were naturally concerned about the loyalty of resident aliens. A foreign element in the population might side with Egypt's enemies in the event of conflict. From the Egyptian viewpoint it was a matter of self-preservation that dictated a policy of anti-semitism.

The Egyptians, however, did not want to drive the Israelites out of the country. Their flocks and herds could provide dainties for the tables of aristocratic Egyptians, and the Israelites themselves comprised a labor force that could be utilized in the royal building projects.

The government decided to build a series of store cities as repositories for provisions and weapons which might be needed in the event of attack upon the eastern Delta. Since the Israelites were living nearby, it seemed wise to put them to work on these cities. Pithom, the first store city mentioned in Exodus (1:11), is the Egyptian *Per-itm,* "house of (the god) Atum," in the Wadi Tumilat, the fertile depression which runs

Brickmaking in Egypt. A wall painting from the tomb of Rekhmire at Thebes (ca. 1450 B.C.) shows slaves making bricks. Israelites did such work in the Delta cities of Pithom and Raamses. Courtesy, The Metropolitan Museum of Art

through the desert separating the Delta from Ismailia. Scholars differ concerning the identification of Pithom, suggesting either Tell el-Mashkhuta ("mound of idols") or Tell er-Retabeh.

Raamses, the second store city, is the Egyptian *Per-Raamses,* "the house of Rameses" where Rameses II (1290-1224 B.C.) maintained his residence. Since the excavations of Pierre Montet at Tanis, most scholars agree that Raamses was located at or near Tanis, the Zoan of Psalm 78:12, 43, and the Avaris of Hyksos times. A letter of a scribe of the Nineteenth Dynasty reveals the impression Raamses made on an Egyptian:

> I have arrived at Per-Raamses the Beloved of Amon, and find that it is most excellent, a magnificent place that has no equal. The god Re has founded it according to the plan of Thebes. To sojourn there is a benefit to life; its fields are full of every good thing, it has foodstuffs and provisions every day. Its pools are full of fish, its lagoons full of birds, its meadows green with grass . . . its fruits have the flavor of honey in the cultivated fields (?). Its granaries are full of barley and grain; they rise up to the sky. It has onions and leeks for foodstuffs (?), pomegranites, apples, and olives and figs from the orchards. Sweet wine from Kenkeme that is more excellent than honey . . . the Shi-hor (i.e. the Pelusiac Branch of the Nile) furnishes salt and nitrate: its boats depart and return. Foodstuffs and provisions are there every day. There one enjoys living, and no one exclaims. Ah yes! The lowly are treated there like the great — Arise, let us celebrate its festivities of heaven and its beginning of summer.

The ruling Pharaoh hoped that the forced labor imposed upon the Israelites would weaken them and check their rapid growth. His plans were frustrated, however, for the more they were oppressed the more they multiplied (Exod. 1:12). It became necessary to try a different strategy.

To limit population growth, the Pharaoh instructed the two midwives who attended the Israelite mothers to kill any male children that were born. In preparation for childbirth, women crouched on a pair of bricks or stones, the "birthstools" mentioned in Exodus (1:16). An Egyptian text preserved in the Papyrus Westcar (*ca.* 1700-1600 B.C.) tells how three goddesses delivered a priest's wife of three sons. Each goddess took a child in her arms. In turn they cut the umbilical cord, washed the child, put it on a little brick bench, and went to the waiting husband to announce the birth. If such a ritual was practiced in the Israelite homes it would have been between the birth of a son and the announcement of the event to the waiting husband that the midwives were asked to kill the child.

The midwives, however, "feared God" (Exod. 1:17) and refused to commit murder even at the command of the Pharaoh. They gave as their excuse that the strong Hebrew women would give birth to their children before the midwife could arrive.

When the Pharaoh learned that he could not work through the midwives to control the Israelite population he determined to go directly to the people. By royal decree it was ordered that every Israelite male child should be cast into the Nile.

4

THE PREPARATION OF MOSES

Into the home of a pious couple of the tribe of Levi a child was born who, according to Pharaoh's decree, should have been cast into the Nile River to perish. The parents, however, like the pious midwives who had defied the royal edict, determined to save their child. For three months Jochebed watched over her infant son, keeping him from prying eyes, and she came to love him more and more each day. As the boy grew older she knew that she could not keep her secret, so she determined to save him by outwitting the king. She placed him in an ark of bulrushes in the Nile and trusted God to care for the child.

An older sister, Miriam, was watching the child in his strange bed when Pharaoh's daughter came to the river to bathe. Jochebed must have known of her habits, and trusted that her sympathy would be aroused by the helpless child. According to plan the princess saw the child and determined to save him. When Miriam saw the princess' interest she offered to find a nurse to care for the child. And so it happened that, in the providence of God, Miriam arranged for Moses' mother to care for her own son with the blessing of Pharaoh's daughter.

The fascinating story of Moses in the bulrushes has parallels in the literature of other peoples. Sargon of Akkad, the Semitic empire builder who ruled much of western Asia during the twenty-fourth century B.C., had a similar experience. Legend says that he was born of a priestess who placed him in a reed basket on the Euphrates River. Akki, a worker on the canals, found the infant and adopted him as his own. The foundling later became the world conqueror who was the first ruler of the dynasty of Akkad (*ca.* 2360-2180 B.C.) .

Although both Sargon and Moses were placed in baskets and taken to rivers, other circumstances of their infancy were quite dissimilar. Sargon's mother wanted to rid herself of an unwanted child, while Moses' mother wished to protect her son from mortal danger. Moses did not, like Sargon, grow up to be a king, but rather became a prophet of God, a deliverer from tyranny, and a lawgiver.

Who was the Pharaoh's daughter who found Moses? The question is related to matters of chronology, and no definite answer can be given. The church historian Eusebius[1] records a tradition that her name was Merris whereas the rabbinical traditions suggest Bityah. Josephus calls her Thermutis.[2]

While there is no evidence to indicate the spot where the child was found, the general locale can be identified with little difficulty. It was near both a royal palace — where Pharaoh's daughter resided — and the place where the Hebrews lived, described elsewhere as the Land of Goshen (Gen. 47:6, 11). This limits the location to the eastern Delta, perhaps near Tanis or Bubastis.

The name Moses seems to be of Egyptian origin. Although the Hebrew form of the word is a play on words, signifying one who is "drawn out" of the water (Exod. 2:10), the Egyptian name goes back to *mes, mesu,* meaning "one born," "a child." A name such as Thothmes means "child (or one born) of Thoth." The name Moses may be a shortened form of a once longer Egyptian word.

Scripture gives no details concerning the youth of Moses. We know that Pharaoh's daughter adopted him and gave him an education such as an Egyptian prince might receive (cf. Acts 7:22). The Egyptian school system was a highly developed one. Sons of tributary princes from the Syro-Palestinian city states were sent to Egypt to study with Egyptian royalty. In this way they became pro-Egyptian in politics, and when a throne was vacant, the rulers of Egypt sought to place one of these Egyptian-trained vassals in the position of power. The boys also served as hostages, for the king of a city state would hardly attack an Egyptian garrison if he thought his own son might suffer as a result. During Moses' period of schooling he may have had classmates from as far north as the Euphrates River, and he may have learned quite a bit about geography and history from them.

Egyptian learning at the middle of the second millennium B.C. was at a high level in such centers as On (Heliopolis) nineteen miles north of the earlier capital, Memphis. The Sep-

1. *Praeparatio evangelica* ix. 27.
2. *Antiquities* II. ix. 5.

tuagint actually mentions Heliopolis along with Pithom and Raamses as cities where the Israelites performed slave labor, and Manetho, the Egyptian historian, claims that Moses became a priest at Heliopolis. Herodotus, known in the West as "the Father of History," observed that the priests at Heliopolis were well informed concerning historical matters. Some generations before Moses, Joseph married Asenath, a daughter of Potiphera, a priest at Heliopolis.

Circumstantial evidence would lead us to think that the education of Moses would take him to a place such as Heliopolis. Temples were usually the depositories for records and royal decrees, and the priests would have access to materials which would not normally be available to laymen.

Probably Moses' first task as a student was the mastery of the hieroglyphic system of writing. The name hieroglyphic (literally "sacred writing") is of Greek origin and it suggests that the priests were the first masters of the art of written communication. Hieroglyphic texts date back well over a millennium and a half before the time of Moses, but only the educated priest or scribe had the ability to read and write.

The Rosetta Stone. Discovered during Napoleon's ill-fated Egyptian campaign, the tri-lingual Rosetta Stone provided the key to the decipherment of Egyptian hieroglyphs. The French Egyptologist, Champollion, published his dissertation on hieroglyphic writing, based on the Rosetta Stone, in 1822. Modern Egyptology had its origin in the work of Champollion and his colleagues.   Courtesy, British Museum

In addition to the hieroglyphs, Moses probably learned to read the Akkadian cuneiform method of writing on clay tablets. Akkadian was the lingua franca of the Amarna Age (fifteenth and fourteenth centuries B.C.). Rulers of the city states in Syria and Palestine as well as kings from the Tigris-Euphrates region corresponded with Egyptian Pharoahs in Akkadian cuneiform. Moses also may have become familiar with the proto-Sinaitic alphabetic script which was used in the turquoise mines at Serabit el-Khadem near Mount Sinai.

A prince such as Moses would have studied the maxims of Ptah-hotep and other sages who gave Egypt a reputation for wisdom in the ancient world. When the Biblical historian wished to extoll the wisdom of King Solomon he said, ". . . Solomon's wisdom surpassed the wisdom of all the people of the east, and all the wisdom of Egypt" (I Kings 4:30). Long before Solomon, the wise men of Egypt sought to instruct the younger generation in prudence and decorum so that they could serve their country in the best possible way.

As an Egyptian prince, Moses would have grown accustomed to the skillful music of court harpists and the sound of handmaids reading aloud the stories which had become a part of Egypt's literary heritage. He probably knew by heart the story of Sinuhe, an Egyptian courtier who left his homeland and spent years among the bedouin of the Syro-Palestinian country until he reached old age and was welcomed back to the wonderful land of Egypt.

Yet at some time in his life Moses learned that he was not an Egyptian. He grew increasingly resentful of the way in which the Egyptians treated his own people. As he visited royal construction projects he heard the sound of the taskmaster's whip and the cries of his kinsmen. Scripture gives no hint of the struggle that must have gone on in Moses' soul during those years. Should he forget his oppressed people and seek fame and office among the people who had adopted him? As the son of Pharaoh's daughter might he even succeed one day to the throne? While we do not know what went on in Moses' mind, we do know the choice that he made: "By faith, Moses, when he was grown up, refused to be called the son of Pharaoh's daughter, choosing rather to share ill-treatment with the people of God than to enjoy the fleeting pleasures of sin" (Heb. 11:24-25).

The Bible does not tell us if the Hebrews ever resorted to violence in their quarrel with Pharaoh. Perhaps passive resistance was their only weapon besides prayer. Once Moses, however, did resort to violence, and the act changed his whole history and that of his people. Seeing an Egyptian taskmaster mistreating a Hebrew slave, Moses intervened and slew the Egyptian. Whatever questions he had in his mind before that act, afterwards there was no turning back. The slaying of the Egyptian might have passed unnoticed had Moses not later tried to intervene in a dispute between two Israelites. When an angry Israelite challenged Moses' right to intervene, mentioning the episode of the slain Egyptian, Moses knew that it would not be safe for him to stay in Egypt.

In fleeing into the eastern wilderness, Moses probably took the same road as Sinuhe, the hero of the story he had known from youth. Sinuhe had fled Egypt seven centuries before Moses, and his journey took him all the way to Syria, while Moses remained in the territory of the Midianites, probably in the Sinai Peninsula. Both refugees found a welcome among nomadic peoples, and both might well have continued to live in prosperity among an alien people. Here, however, the similarity ends. Sinuhe returned to Egypt because he was desirous of spending his last days in the land of his birth. Moses returned because Yahweh had commissioned him to lead his suffering kinsmen to freedom.

Moses' years in Midian were not wasted. After helping the seven daughters of a Midianite priest to water their flocks, Moses was invited to live with the priest, and ultimately he married one of the daughters (Exod. 2:18; 3:1). Moses seems to have had a happy time with Jethro (or Reuel), his father-in-law. During the years of his sojourn in Midian, Zipporah, Moses' wife, bore two sons — Gershom and Eliezer (Exod. 2:11-22; 18:4).

When the Pharaoh, who had ruled Egypt at the time Moses slew the Egyptian, had died (Exod. 2:23a), Israel hoped for deliverance from the oppression. God heard the prayers of his people and appeared to Moses in the midst of a burning bush, identifying Himself as the God of Abraham, Isaac, and Jacob (Exod. 3). Moses was to become the leader of his people, rescuing them from Egyptian bondage and bringing them back to the land of their fathers. God instructed Moses to demand that Pharaoh permit the Israelites to go a three day journey into the wilderness to sacrifice. When Moses insisted that he did not have eloquence for the task, God stated that Aaron his brother could be his spokesman (Exod. 4:14-16). Moses was also armed with two signs: a rod which could be transformed into a serpent, and a hand which would turn leprous when placed in his bosom (Exod. 4:1-9).

On the way back from Midian to Egypt a strange event took place. At a lodging place along the way the Lord met Moses and, in the words of Exodus 4:24, sought to kill him. Moses was evidently very sick, so his wife Zipporah took a flint and circumcised her son. For some unexplained reason Moses had not performed the rite of circumcision, which was the seal of the covenant made between the Lord and Abraham. After the circumcision, Moses recovered from his sickness and continued the journey.

Aaron joined Moses (Exod. 4:27), and Moses shared with his brother the experience which he had had in the wilderness. Aaron in turn recounted God's mighty acts to the elders of Israel, and they and the people knew that God was about to answer their prayers by sending deliverance.

Copper Mining in the Negeb. The Promised Land was described as a land "out of whose hills thou mayest dig copper" (Deut. 8:9). Israeli miners still work the copper mines.   Courtesy, Consulate General of Israel

5

THE TEN PLAGUES AND THE PASSOVER

When Moses appeared before Pharaoh, demanding that Israel be permitted to sacrifice in the wilderness, Pharaoh asked contemptuosuly, "Who is Yahweh?" To the proud ruler of Egypt, the God of the Israelites was but one god among many, and certainly inferior to the gods of Egypt. Moses and Aaron identified Yahweh as the God of the Hebrews, affirming that his people were required to offer sacrifices in the wilderness lest their God be displeased and bring a plague upon them.

Pharaoh, however, showed no flexibility. Not only would he not allow them to go to the wilderness, but he insisted that their work load be increased. They would not be provided straw as a binding material for the bricks they produced, but they would still have to produce the same number of bricks each day.

The bad news of Pharaoh's despotism was countered by good news from the God of Israel. God assured his people that deliverance was at hand. Moses and Aaron went before Pharaoh. Aaron cast down the rod which had been given him as a symbol of God's authority and power. The rod became a serpent. Thereupon the Egyptian magicians, traditionally named Jannes and Jambres (cf. II Tim. 3:6-8), performed a similar feat in an attempt to discredit Moses. In imitating this miracle they may have made use of the art of snake charming. When rendered completely insensible, a snake will appear as still as a rod. "But Aaron's rod swallowed up their rods" (Exod. 7:12). In this way the God of Israel demonstrated his power over the wisest of the Egyptians and their gods.

When Pharaoh refused to acknowledge the claims of the God of Israel, he and the entire land of Egypt suffered a series of ten plagues. Except for the last — the death of the first born — none of the plagues was completely strange to Egypt. The timing of the plagues — at the word of Moses — and their intensity constituted the miraculous element. The Bible consistently presents Yahweh as sovereign over all creation. The forces of nature are always subject to his control.

The distinction made between the Israelites in Goshen and the Egyptians in the Nile Valley underscored the concern of Israel's God for his people. From one viewpoint the plagues were a chapter in Moses' contest with Pharaoh; from a second viewpoint they represent the challenge of Yahweh to the gods of Egypt.

When Moses, at the command of God, stretched his rod over the Nile waters they became red and putrid (Exod. 7:14-25). This plague reflects conditions brought about by an unusually high Nile, which normally reaches flood stage in August. The waters are then saturated with finely powered red earth from basins of the Blue Nile and Atbara, and they carry along minute organisms which help to color the water and create conditions so unfavorable for the fish that they die in large numbers. It may be that the extreme intensification of this phenomenon as described in Exodus 7:21, occurring at the word of Moses, produced the first plague which lasted seven days. Pharaoh, however, was unmoved by the scourge which should have convinced him of Yahweh's power.

When Moses again approached Pharaoh and he refused to let Israel go, God told Moses to stretch forth his rod over the waters, and there came forth from the waters, an army of frogs which invaded the land in such numbers that they became a national catastrophe (Exod. 8:1-15). Frogs are not unusual in the Nile Valley. The plague of frogs, however, came at the word of Moses and was of such intensity the Pharaoh should have recognized the power of Yahweh. When the frogs died in large numbers the land again was filled with the odor of decaying flesh. But Pharaoh remained unmoved and refused to let Israel go as Moses had requested.

Heaps of decaying frogs and fish provide an ideal breeding ground for insect pests. At the word of the Lord, Moses stretched forth his rod and smote the dust, and there came forth a large number of insects variously described as gnats, lice or mosquitoes (Exod. 8:16-19). This was, as the third plague, God's third warning to Pharaoh and challenge to Egypt's gods.

While the Egyptian magicians had been successful in imitating the first two miracles, we read that when they tried to bring forth lice "They could not" (Exod. 8:14). We can only speculate why this might have been. Nor do we read of the magicians seeking to imitate the subsequent miracles. Instead they give up with the report to Pharaoh "This is the finger of God" (Exod. 8:15).

Next followed the plague of flies (Exod. 8:20-32), probably the *Stomoxys calcitrans* which was an evil itself, and brought disease in its wake. This was the first plague in which God made a distinction between the Israelites and the Egyptians (Exod. 8:19). The Israelites were safe in Goshen, and the plague did not reach them there.

The fifth plague, a plague upon Egypt's cattle (Exod. 9:1-7), had religious as well as economic overtones. The goddess Hathor was represented as a bull, and the Apis Bull had for centuries been one of the objects of veneration throughout Egypt. Yahweh struck at the heart of Egyptian religious life in bringing a plague on the cattle.

The sixth plague (Exod. 9:8-12) struck human beings and animals with boils. These may have been produced by the same carrier flies that spread disease among the cattle. But again the plague was confined to the Egyptians. Yahweh preserved his people from affliction in Goshen.

As the seventh plague God used a disastrous hailstorm (Exod. 10:1-20). "Only in the land of Goshen, where the children of Israel were, was there no hail" (Exod. 9:26). This took place at the end of January or the beginning of February, for the barley and flax were ruined, but the wheat and spelt had not yet grown up (Exod. 9:31-32).

We now read for the first time that Pharaoh acknowledged his sin in not letting Israel go. And, recognizing that Moses was God's intermediary, he asked Moses to entreat Yahweh to cause the storm to cease. Moses "spread abroad his hands to the Lord; and the thunders and hail ceased . . ." (Exod. 9:33).

Next, probably in March, locusts in unprecedented numbers swooped into Egypt and ate whatever vegetation had survived the earlier plagues (Exod. 10:1-20). Pharaoh once more acknowledged his sin and begged Moses to "entreat the Lord," and when Moses entreated the Lord, God sent a mighty west wind which swept the locusts into the Red Sea (Exod. 10:18, 19).

In the ninth plague thick darkness (Exod. 10:21-29) covered the land. Dust storms, known as *Khamsin,* are common in Egypt. Masses of earth, brought down the Nile Valley at the time of the annual inundation, dry into a fine powder. Such storms frequently come in March and last about three days (cf. Exod. 10:23). When the *Khamsin* wind comes, dust fills the air.

In the ninth plague the darkness was so intense that the sun itself seemed to be blotted out. "But all the children of Israel had light in their dwellings" (Exod. 10:23).

The plagues represent God's judgment on the gods of Egypt (cf. Exod. 12:12). Ha^cpi, the Nile god had brought stench and ruin instead of blessing. Frogs, associated with the gods of fruitfulness, brought disease instead of life. The light of the sun (Re) was blotted out during the plague of darkness. Yahweh desired Egypt as well as Israel to know His power.

The last plague, the death of Egypt's firstborn, was Egypt's darkest hour but it marked the beginning of Israel's deliverance. To protect Israel in time of plague, God ordered the head of each household to slay a lamb (Exod. 12:1-6) and to sprinkle its blood on the lintel and doorposts of the house (Exod. 12:7). The roast lamb was then to be eaten in haste, each Israelite having his loins girded, sandals on his feet, and his staff in his hand (Exod. 12:11). Israel was to be prepared to leave in haste, for this was to be their last night in Egypt.

When the death angel passed through Egypt, the first born of man and beast died, but the blood upon the Israelite houses was a sign which the angel honored. God said, "The blood shall be a sign for you, upon the houses where you are; and when I see the blood, I will pass over you, and no plague shall fall upon you to destroy you when I smite the land of Egypt." (Exod. 12:13). The Passover took place on the tenth day of Abib, or Nisan, which corresponds to our March-April. It was to become an annual festival in which God's people would celebrate their deliverance from Egypt. Passover was a family festival, presided over by the father of the house (Exod. 12:3-4), although in later years it came to be associated with the Jerusalem Temple (cf. II Chron. 30:1-27; 35:1-19). In New Testament times the paschal victim was ritually slaughtered in the Temple but the Passover meal could be eaten in any house within the bounds of Jerusalem. After the destruction of the Temple (A.D. 70), the Passover again became a family festival, observed in Jewish homes throughout the world.

Closely associated with the Passover ceremony was the Feast of Unleavened Bread (Exod. 12:14-20; Lev. 23:5-8), and eventually they became one eight day festival — the twenty-four hour Passover observance followed by seven days of the Feast of Unleavened Bread. The unleavened bread is called "the bread of affliction" in Deuteronomy 16:3, because the Israelites ate it in haste before leaving Egypt.

At the midnight hour when death struck the first-born of Egypt, Pharaoh sent for Moses and urged him to take his people away (Exod. 12:29-32). Moses, the Israelites, a mixed multitude that accompanied them, flocks and herds left Raamses on the first step of the journey to Canaan. They took with them the silver and gold jewelry which their Egyptian neighbors gave them (Exod. 12:35-36) and the bones of Joseph who had asked his brothers to swear that they would carry his bones back to Canaan at the time that God would bring them back to the land of promise (Exod. 13:19; cf. Gen. 50:24, 25).

6

FROM EGYPT TO SINAI

The Sinai Peninsula, which Israel entered after crossing the Red Sea, comprises the barren wilderness south of the land bridge which connects Egypt with Palestine. The Brook of Egypt, known today as the Wadi El-Arish, flowing northward from the Wilderness of Paran, marks the geographical boundary between the two countries. It is but a short distance from Egypt to Palestine. Kantara, in the eastern Delta is but one hundred seventeen miles from Raphia in southern Canaan. The Roman general Titus took just five days to march his army from Sile in Egypt to Gaza.

The Peninsula itself is triangular in shape, two hundred sixty miles long and one hundred fifty miles wide at the north, where a belt of sandy soil fifteen miles deep stretches along the Mediterranean Coast. South of this coastal plain is a high gravel and limestone plateau which stretches southward one hundred and fifty miles. Beyond the plateau, at the apex of the Peninsula, is a granite mountain formation with peaks reaching as high as eight thousand feet above sea level. This is the region of the copper and turquoise mines which were exploited by the Egyptians since the third millennium before Christ.

Traffic eastward from Egypt had a choice of three roads, The most direct route was the *Via Maris,* "the way of the sea," which skirted the Mediterranean. It began at the frontier fortress of Sile, near modern Qantara, and reached Canaan at Raphia. Pharaoh Seti I (1308-1290 B.C.) built a series of fortifications along this route which was used by the armies of Egypt when they campaigned in Asia. The Egyptians named the road, "The Way of Horus," but Scripture calls it "The Way of the Land of the Philistines" (Exod. 13:17-18), asserting that the Israelites avoided this direct road into Canaan at the direction of God. Pharaoh's former slaves were in no condition to wage full-scale warfare, which would have been unavoidable had they chosen to use the direct coastal road.

South of the *Via Maris* was the "Way to Shur" over which Hagar had fled from her mistress Sarah during patriarchal times (Gen. 16:7). Hagar, an Egyptian, was evidently on the way home when an angel stopped her and told her to return to Abraham and Sarah. The Egyptians had built a wall at their eastern frontier to control caravan traffic and the migration of nomads. Shur, a name meaning "wall" was probably the name of the town which grew up around the check point garrisoned by Egyptian border guards near modern Ismailia on the Suez Canal. The "Way to Shur" crossed the Sinai Peninsula from southern Canaan where it connected with the important water-parting route from Jerusalem and Hebron to Beer-sheba in the Negeb.

A third route, known in modern times as "the Pilgrim's Way," *Darb el-Haj,* runs across the Peninsula from the head of the Gulf of Suez to Ezion-geber (Elat) at the head of the Gulf of Aqaba. The two gulfs — Suez and Aqaba — extend like rabbit ears in a northwesterly and northeasterly direction bounding the Sinai Peninsula.

Although it is clear that the Exodus did not take Israel along any well-traveled road it is difficult for modern geographers to trace the route with any certainty. Scripture calls it the "Reed Sea" or Wilderness Route, but the precise location of the crossing of the Reed Sea is not known. Near the town of Raamses are two bodies of water: the Water of Horus (Shihor in Isa. 23:3) and the Papyrus Marsh, a name similar in meaning to the Biblical "Reed Sea." Scripture states that the Exodus began at Raamses in the eastern Delta (Num. 33:5), a town identified with Egyptian *Per-Ramses,* the capital which Rameses II built at or near the site of ancient Tanis. It was in this region that the patriarch Jacob had settled some centuries before (Gen. 47:11) when it was described as "the choicest part of the land."

The fleeing Israelites made stops at Succoth, modern *Tell el-Mashkutah,* in the eastern part of the Wadi Tumilat, and at Etham "on the edge of the wilderness" (Exod. 13:20). From Etham, possibly a frontier fortress where they encountered difficulty, the Israelites turned northward to Pi-hahiroth (Exod. 14:2, 9). The Israelite encampment is described as: "at the sea, by Pi-hahiroth, in front of Baal-zephon" (Exod. 14:9). Clear as these geographical references must have been to ancient readers, modern scholarship has had difficulty understanding their meaning. Baal-zephon is a Semitic name meaning, "Baal of the North." This deity, originally adopted in Egypt from Canaanite sources, was worshiped in many places in Lower Egypt. A letter from the sixth century B.C. mentions "Baal-zephon and all the gods of Tahpanhes," suggesting to many scholars that a Baal-zephon temple was located at Tahpanhes, modern Tell Defneh, about twenty-seven miles south-southwest of Port Said.[1] W. F. Albright would locate Baal-zephon in the region of the later Egyptian town of Tahpanhes to which Jeremiah fled around 586 B.C. (Jer. 43) along with his countrymen who feared reprisals from Nebuchadnezzar after the slaying of Gedaliah. Herodotus states that Pharaoh Psammetichus I (664-610 B.C.) established a colony of Greek mercenaries there. In Hellenistic times the town boasted a temple to Zeus Casius, the Greek equivalent of Baal-zephon, which stood on the narrow strip of land bordering Lake Sirbonis to the north.

Migdol is a common Semitic place name, meaning "tower." The Egyptian wall must have had many towers, but it is unlikely that many bore Semitic names. We read of a Migdol of Seti later called the Migdol of Merneptah, modern Tell el Heir south of Pelusium in the northern sector of the wall. This seems to be that area from which Israel left Egypt at the Exodus.

The Pharaoh decided to pursue the escaping Israelites before they reached the Reed Sea and came upon them with his chariots in the region of Pi-hahiroth, possibly one of the canals linking the various lakes reaching to the Nile in this region. The approach of Pharaoh's chariots struck terror in the hearts of the escaping Israelites (Exod. 14:10-18). Moses encouraged them to trust the Lord, and he, at God's command, lifted his rod in the direction of the Reed Sea, whereupon God sent a strong east wind which divided the sea so that the people could cross over on dry land. The miracle was one of timing. At the moment Moses raised his rod, the wind drove back the waters of the sea so that Israel could cross over. The Egyptian chariots attempted to follow, but their chariot wheels were clogged and when Moses stretched his hand over the sea a second time, the waters returned and covered Pharaoh's host (Exod. 14:26-31). Moses led the people in a song of triumph (Exod. 15:1-17) and his sister Miriam exclaimed:

Sing to the Lord for He has triumphed gloriously;
The horse and his rider he has thrown into the sea. (Exod. 15:21)

---

1. Cf. William F. Albright, BASOR, 109 (1948), pp. 15-16.

Traditionally the name of the sea which Israel crossed in its exodus from Egypt has been known as the Red Sea, although the Hebrew name *Yam Suph* is clearly, "sea of reeds." The term aptly describes the lake region north of the Gulf of Suez comprising the Bitter Lakes and Lake Timsah. It is possible that the Israelites went along the narrow neck of land on which Baal-zephon stood and that the Biblical Sea of Reeds was modern Lake Sirbonis. We are certain that the crossing was in this area because the Israelites found themselves in the Wilderness of Shur after crossing the sea (Exod. 15:22). The Wilderness of Shur is in the northwestern part of the Sinai Peninsula extending from the Wadi el Arish (the Biblical "River of Egypt") to the modern Suez Canal. All of the direct routes from Egypt to Canaan passed through the Wilderness of Shur.

Instead of taking one of the direct routes eastward, the Israelites turned southward into the Sinai Peninsula, taking a route parallel to the Gulf of Suez. A brief stop was made at Marah, an oasis where the water was bitter until Moses threw a tree into the water making it sweet (Exod. 15:22-25). Marah is often identified with ᶜAin Hawara several miles inland from the Gulf of Suez. G. E. Wright prefers ᶜAin Musa, or an unknown spring near the Bitter Lakes since ᶜAin Hawara is hard to reconcile with a three day journey from the Reed Sea (Exod. 15:22). The second stop was at Elim, a word meaning "terebinths" or "oaks." The Israelites were refreshed by its twelve springs and seventy palm trees (Exod. 15:27). Although we cannot be certain concerning its location, it may have been the Wadi Gharandel about forty miles south southeast of Suez along the west side of the Sinai Peninsula. Israel continued to move southward along the Gulf of Suez. The next encampment according to Numbers 33:10 was "by the Sea of Reeds," a term here evidently used of the Gulf of Suez. The fifteenth century Egyptian port of Merkhah, situated five miles south of Ras Abu Zeneimeh has been suggested for the place of encampment.

About six weeks after the Exodus from Egypt, Israel entered the Wilderness of Sin (Exod. 16:1), usually identified with Debbet er-Ramleh, a sandy section of the southwestern Sinai Peninsula (Exod. 16:1). Here the people murmured against Moses and Aaron, and God miraculously provided manna to sustain them (Exod. 16:4-12). The Israelites were instructed to gather an omer apiece for five days, and two omers on the sixth day to provide food for the sabbath (Exod. 16:16-21). The word "manna" means, "What is it?" the question which the Israelites asked when they first saw it. Scripture states that manna was "like coriander seed, white, and the taste of it was like wafers made with honey" (Exod. 16:31).

Many scholars identify manna with the excretions of insects on tamarisk trees each June. At night drops of the secretion fall to the ground where they remain until ants consume them. These drops are small, sticky, light in color, and sugary sweet. The fact that it was provided but six days a week and that it continued to nourish the Israelites until they arrived in Canaan, after forty years in the wilderness, indicates that manna cannot be explained on purely natural bases. The modern parallel to Biblical manna, still gathered in the Sinai peninsula, can at best suggest the means that God used in feeding his people.

At least twice during the wilderness wandering God provided quail to augment the diet of his people (Exod. 16:13; Num. 11:31). Quail cross the Mediterranean in September and October to winter in Arabia or Africa, and they migrate northward again in the spring. As the quail blew in from the sea, the Israelites "spread them out all around the camp" (Num. 11:32). In describing the customs of the Egyptians, Herodotus notes: "They eat fish uncooked, either dried in the sun or preserved with brine. Quails and ducks and small birds are salted and eaten raw."[2]

In leaving the Wilderness of Sin, the Israelites made a stop at Dophkah (Num. 33:12), near the copper and turquoise mines which were operated by Pharaohs from early dynastic times. In the center of the mining region was the famed temple of the goddess Hathor at Serabit el-Khadem. Hundreds of ancient inscriptions have been identified at the temple and at the entrances to the mines. Although most of them are in hieroglyphic Egyptian characters, about forty are in the so-called Proto-Sinaitic alphabetic script of the fifteenth century B.C. The mines were probably not in use at the time the Israelites passed through Dophkah.

The last stop before Mount Sinai was at Rephidim (Exod. 17:1), possibly modern Wadi Refayid in the Wilderness of Sinai. Here the people murmured against Moses because they lacked water. God instructed him to meet their need by using his rod to strike the rock (Exod. 17:6). He did so and water miraculously flowed from the smitten rock. C. S. Jarvis tells of a camel corps digging for water which had an experience

2. Herodotus, *Histories* i. 77.

analagous to that of Moses. A hammer accidentally hit a rock
and water came out from the rock itself. The polished hard
surface of the limestone covered soft porous rock from which
the water flowed. Such parallels may be useful in showing the
means that God used in meeting the needs of His people, but
they do not diminish the need for God's miraculous intervention to sustain Israel in its wilderness journey.

At Rephidim Israel encountered hostilities for the first time.
Nomadic Amalekites attacked the encampment (Exod. 17:8-13),
but thanks to the intercession of Moses, assisted by Aaron and
Hur, and the valor of Joshua who appears in Scripture for the
first time as a mighty warrior, Israel prevailed. The Amalekites
continued to be bitter enemies of the Israelites in the period
of the Judges (Judg. 3:13) and of the monarchy (I Sam. 27:6;
30:1-20).

Jethro, Moses' father-in-law who had provided a home and a
wife for Moses during his years in the wilderness, joined Moses
again before the Israelites reached Mount Sinai. Jethro re-
joiced in the success of Israel and paid tribute to Moses' God,
offering a burnt offering and other sacrifices (Exod. 18:10-12).
He also gave practical advice when he noted that Moses was
overworked. Moses was attempting to handle all the detail for
the encampment, whereas Jethro suggested that he appoint able
men to assist in governing the people (Exod. 18:13-27).

Three months after the Exodus, Israel reached the wilderness
of Sinai and encamped before the mountain of the same name
(Exod. 19:1). Geographers are far from unanimous, however,
concerning the identity of Mount Sinai. Tradition since the
latter part of the fourth century has located Sinai in the southern part of the Sinai Peninsula. Legend states that Catherine
of Alexandria, after her martyrdom, was carried by angels to
the top of the mountain that now bears her name. A monastery
has been located there continuously since the fourth century,
although the Christians have undergone periods of severe persecution. The Moslem conquest brought with it anti-Christian
feeling, but the monastery had already undergone persecution
in the days of St. Nilus (A.D. 390) and the monk Ammonius
(A.D. 373). The present Monastery of Saint Catherine, on the
northwest slope of Jebel Musa, a 6,500 foot high mountain, was
founded about A.D. 527 under Emperor Justinian who established it on the site where Helena, the mother of Constantine,
had erected a small church two centuries earlier.

Approaching Jebel Musa ("Mount Moses") from Serabit el-

The Traditional Mount Sinai. Jebel Musa (Arabic for Mount Moses), in the southern part of the Sinai Peninsula is the traditional Mount Sinai or Horeb where Moses received the Law.   Courtesy, Matson Photo Service

Khadem, the traveler enters a wide valley called er-Raha, two miles long and one-third to two-thirds of a mile wide. This would have been a natural place for Israel to have encamped (Exod. 19:1-2; Num. 33:15). Towering above the plain are three summits, Ras es-Safsaf to the northwest, Jebel Musa to the southeast, and, still higher, Jebel Katarin rising 9,000 feet to the southwest. While Jebel Musa is the favored location we cannot be positive concerning the original Sinai. Ras es-Safsaf is closer to the plain and is favored by some scholars for that reason (cf. Exod. 20:18). The church historian Eusebius preferred still another site, Jebel Serbel west of the Wadi Feiran, and some scholars abandon the Sinai Peninsula entirely, suggesting a site in northwestern Arabia or in the vicinity of Kadesh-barnea. The imposing granite formations of the southern Sinai Peninsula are still preferred, however, as the site for Mount Sinai where Moses received the Law.

7

THE ENCAMPMENT AT SINAI

The third month after their departure from Egypt, the Israelites encamped before the sacred mount. Moses commanded the people to prepare themselves for three days and forbade anyone to go up the mountain under penalty of death. On the third day, amidst lightning, thunder, and thick clouds, Moses ascended the mountain and received the divine Law (Exod. 19:16-20). A second time accompanied by Joshua, he went up the mountain. Forty days and nights he communed with God, during which time he received additional commandments (Exod. 24:1-15).

Upon entering the cloud-covered mountain Moses received the Book of the Covenant which was to regulate Israel's religious life. When the people expressed their willingness to observe its precepts, Moses sprinkled the blood of sacrificial animals upon the altar which he had erected and upon the people. By this act God and Israel were effectually joined together and the Covenant became binding. God would henceforth be Israel's God, and Israel would be His people.

The first of the Ten Commandments specifies that Yahweh is the God of His people, and that they are to have no other gods aside from him. This command is not an absolute assertion of monotheism, but monotheism is germinally present. From the practical point of view, the commandments had to reckon with many deities. The Israelites themselves were conscious that their fathers had worshiped other gods (cf. Gen. 35:2). They had been in Egypt where a complex polytheism was accepted as the national religion. They would soon be in Canaan where the fertility cult would hold sway. In such a context it was necessary to affirm a strict monolatry — Yahweh, as Israel's God would not tolerate a rival. The fact that these other "gods" were in reality idols, the work of man's hands and man's imagination would later be asserted as monotheism developed philosophically and theologically. The Decalogue dealt with its practical side — no Israelite might worship any God except Yahweh.

The temptation of the ancients — and of many moderns — is to think of God in visible, tangible form. In Egypt the Israelites daily saw the images of birds, beasts, and humans receiving worship. At Sinai Yahweh made it clear that no "graven image or likeness" would be tolerated in religion. Not only must His people not bow down to images of pagan deities, they must make no image of Yahweh, either. The golden calf (Exod. 32:1-6) was a violation of the command, even though it was designed to represent the God who had brought Yahweh's people from Egypt. The calves that Jeroboam set up at Bethel and Dan (I Kings 12:28) are likewise forbidden. Although the theologically mature leaders may have pictured Yahweh as riding the calves, the tendency of such representations was to cause people to identify the deity with the cult object, and it is just that tendency that the decalogue sought to check.

The commandment against the misuse of God's name lays stress on the attribute of holiness. Yahweh had revealed His name to Moses, and Israel, God's people, was warned against a loose use of the divine Name. Israel must not swear at all in the name of a false god, and she must never swear falsely in the name of her own God, Yahweh. Thoughtless vows (such as that of Jephthah, Judg. 11:30-31), cursing, sorcery, soothsaying were all contrary to the intent of the commandment.

Israel had been prepared for the Sabbath commandment by the miracle of the manna. The basis for the Sabbath commandment of Exodus 20:8-11 is that "in six days Yahweh made heaven and earth, the sea and all that is in them, and rested the seventh day." In the repetition of the commandments in Deuteronomy 5, no mention is made of creation, but rather Israel was commanded, "You shall remember that you were a servant in the land of Egypt, and Yahweh your God brought you out thence with a mighty hand and an outstretched arm; therefore Yahweh your God commanded you to keep the sabbath day." The Sabbath is presented as a day of abstaining from labor, and as such it was to become a mark of Israel's loyalty to Yahweh.

The second "table of the Law" is concerned with man's relations with his fellows: children must obey their parents, the sanctity of life must be recognized, the rights of personal property must be respected, man must maintain his integrity as a citizen ("You shall not bear false witness against your neighbor"). Finally, the source of evil in man is underscored. Man must not desire that which is not rightly his. He must respect the marriage relationship and honor his neighbor's right to a happy home with the possessions that God has entrusted to him.

The ceremony by which the union of Israel and Yahweh was accomplished (Exod. 24:3-8) consisted of a covenant ritual. An altar was erected representing the deity, and the people stood opposite. Sacrificial victims were then slain, and their blood was drained off into bowls. Part of the blood was then thrown over the altar, and the rest flung over the heads of the people. Symbolically the life of the victim was used to cover the two contracting parties — Yahweh and Israel. Since both were united in the blood of a third party they were united to one another.

This relationship between Yahweh and Israel was one of election, or choice. Among many ancient Semitic tribes the tribal members thought of themselves as blood descendants of the deity. Israel, however, remembered a time when she was not the people of Yahweh, when her ancestors had worshiped other gods in Ur of the Chaldees. Religion among the patriarchs was highly personal, but at Sinai it became national. Yahweh had not simply pledged himself to be the god of an individual, but of a people. God set his love upon Israel, and Israel voluntarily accepted that love and the covenant which expressed it.

In addition to the Ten Commandments, Moses gave to Israel a series of laws to clarify the application of the Decalogue to the life of God's people (Exod. 20:22 — 23:19). Instructions were given concerning the proper place of sacrifice, the treatment of slaves, and other applications of the law to the circumstances of daily life.

Professor George Mendenhall of the University of Michigan has shown that the form of the Sinai Covenant is paralleled by treaties made between kings and their vassals in the ancient Near East, particularly among the Hittites. Near Eastern literature affords examples of parity covenants, or covenants between equals. Such covenants appear in the Bible between David and Jonathan (I Sam. 20) and between Shechem and Israel (Gen. 34). When a king covenants with a vassal, however, the treaty takes a different form. Such covenants are mentioned in II Samuel 5:1-5 where David covenants with the people as their king, and in I Kings 20:33-34 where Ahab imposes a treaty on the Syrians.

Mendenhall has shown that a typical Hittite suzerainty treaty has six parts which are paralleled in the Mosaic Law. The treaty begins by identifying the sovereign in a form such as, "Thus says X, the Great King." The Biblical decalogue begins with such a line of identification, "I am Yahweh your God" (Exod. 20:2a; Cf. Josh. 24:2). Secondly, the treaty mentions its historical background, speaking of the benevolent actions of the king. In Exodus 20:2b, Yahweh declares that he brought his people "out of the land of Egypt, out of the house of bondage." It is this act of mercy that forms the basis for the third element in the covenant, its stipulations. A Hittite treaty would spell out the obligations of vassals. They would not be permitted to have treaty relations with foreign powers, particularly such as were unfriendly to the Hittites. Yahweh demands of his people, "You shall have no other gods before me" (Exod. 20:3), and again, "Take heed to yourselves, lest you make a covenant with the inhabitants of the land whither you go, lest it become a snare in the midst of you. You shall tear down their altars and break their pillars, and cut down their Asherim (for you shall worship no other god, for Yahweh whose name is Jealous is a jealous God) " (Exod. 34:12-13).

A Hittite covenant was deposited in the sanctuary of the vassal and publicly read at regular intervals. Yahweh instructed Moses, "And you shall put into the ark, the testimony which I shall give you" (Exod. 25:16). This testimony, or law, was to be read every seven years (Deut. 31:9-13). At the time that Solomon built his temple we read, "There was nothing in the ark except the two tables of stone which Moses put there at Horeb, where the Lord made a covenant with the people of Israel when they came out of the land of Egypt" (I Kings 8:9).

A treaty between a Hittite king and his vassals would continue by invoking the deities of the respective parties as witnesses. Israelite monotheism precludes invoking a pantheon, as the heathen did, and since God "had no one greater by whom to swear, he swore by himself" (Heb. 6:13). At the covenant renewal before the death of Joshua, Moses' successor "took up a great stone, and set it there under the oak in the sanctuary of the Lord, and Joshua said to all the people, 'Behold, this stone shall be a witness against us; for it has heard all the words of the Lord which he spoke to us; therefore it shall be a witness against you lest you deal falsely with your God' " (Josh. 24:26, 27).

The treaty would conclude with a list of blessings which

could be expected by those who would keep the covenant faith-
fully, and the curses which would fall upon the violator of
covenant responsibilities. Such lists of blessings and curses appear in Leviticus 26 and Deuteronomy 27 and 28. As a solemn
warning we read, "Cursed be he who does not confirm the
words of this law by doing them" (Deut. 27:26).

Immediately following the ratification of the covenant, Israel
was commanded to construct a portable Tabernacle, or "tent
of meeting" so that God might dwell in the midst of His people (Exod. 25:8). To prepare for the building of this sanctuary,
Moses instructed the people to bring free-will offerings of gold,
silver, bronze; cloth or yarn of blue, purple, and scarlet color;
fine linen; goats' hair; rams' skins; goat skins; acacia wood;
spices for anointing oil and incense; and precious stones for
the ephod and breastplate of the priest (Exod. 25:1-7). The
workmanship was entrusted to a man of the tribe of Judah
named Bezalel who was filled "with the Spirit of God, with
ability and intelligence, with knowledge and all craftsmanship,
to devise artistic designs, to work in gold, silver, and bronze,
in cutting stones for setting and in carving wood, for work in
every craft" (Exod. 31:1-5). Associated with Bezalel was Oholiab
of the tribe of Dan.

The tent of meeting was erected in a court having a perime-
ter of three hundred cubits (450 feet), surrounded by curtains
of fine twined linen hung on bronze pillars, seven and one-half
feet high, with silver hooks. The only entrance was at the east
end, and through it the Israelites were able to approach the
Altar of Burnt Offering (Exod. 27:1-8; 38:1-7). The altar was
made of acacia wood covered with bronze, seven and one-half
feet square and four and one-half feet high with horns pro-
jecting from each corner. Like other parts of the tent of meeting, it was portable and equipped with staves and rings. Beyond
the Altar of Burnt Offering was a bronze laver used by the
priests for ceremonial washing before officiating at the Altar or
in the Tent of Meeting (Exod. 30:17-21; 38:8; 40:30).

In the western half of the court, the Tent of Meeting was
located. It was forty-five feet long, fifteen feet wide, and divided
into two parts. The Tent of Meeting was built of acacia wood
boards overlaid with gold (Exod. 26:1-37; 36:20-38). There
were forty-eight boards in all, twenty for each of the sides and
eight for the west end. They were fifteen feet high, two and
one-quarter feet wide, and held together by bars and sockets.
The ceiling was in the form of a curtain of fine twined linen

of purple, blue, and scarlet cover ornamented with cherubim. The outer covering was made of goat's hair as protection for the linen, and over this, for added protection, were coverings of rams' skins and goats' skins. Two veils of the same material as the first covering were employed: one at the entrance to the Tent of Meeting (at the east end) and the other to separate the two interior rooms, the Holy Place and the Most Holy Place.

The northern part of the Holy Place was occupied by the Table of Shewbread, made of acacia wood overlaid with gold, with a golden rim around the top. A ring was attached to each leg for carrying (Exod. 25:23-30; 37:10-16). On the table were twelve cakes of unleavened bread which were changed each Sabbath, those of the week before being eaten by the priests (Lev. 24:5-9). Plates for incense were also placed on the table.

The Golden Lampstand was placed in the southern part of the Holy Place. It was beaten or hammered from one piece of pure gold (Exod. 25:31-39; 37:17-24) and had a central stem with three curving branches on each side, making seven lamps

The Ark of the Covenant. In Hellenistic and Roman times, Jewish synagogues were ornamented with paintings and sculpture. This representation of the Ark of the Covenant was discovered among ruins of the synagogue at Capernaum (3rd century A.D.).   Courtesy, Israel Office of Information

in all. Snuffers and trays were also made of gold. Every evening the priests filled the lamp with olive oil which had been furnished by the Israelites (Exod. 27:20-21; 30:7-8).

Before the veil separating the Holy Place from the Holy of Holies was the Altar of Incense, three feet high and one and one-half feet square, made of acacia wood overlaid with gold (Exod. 40:22-28). It had a golden border around the top and was equipped with a horn and ring at each corner (Exod. 30:1-10, 28, 34-37). Each morning and evening as the priests came to attend the Golden Lampstand they took fire from the Altar of Burnt Offering in the court, and offered incense at the Altar of Incense in the Holy Place.

Beyond the veil was the Holy of Holies, the throne room of Yahweh. Its central object was the Ark of the Covenant made of acacia wood overlaid within and without with pure gold. The ark was three and three-quarters feet long, two and one-quarter feet deep and wide, equipped with golden rings and staves for carrying (Exod. 25:10-22; 37:1-9). The cover of the ark, known as the Mercy Seat, served as the base for two golden cherubim which faced each other with wings overshadowing the center of the Mercy Seat. Here on the annual Day of Atonement, the High Priest sprinkled blood for the nation of Israel (Lev. 16:14).

Within the Ark of the Covenant were placed the tablets of the Law (Exod. 25:21; 31:18; Deut. 10:3-5), a pot of manna (Exod. 36:34), and Aaron's rod that had blossomed in token of his divine election (Num. 17:10). The Ark of the Covenant was looked upon as Israel's most sacred cult object. After the conquest it was temporarily housed at Shiloh (I Sam. 4:3) whence it was taken by the Israelites to the field of battle as a guarantee of victory over the Philistines. This desecration of the Ark was contrary to God's will, and the Philistines defeated Israel at Aphek and captured the Ark, although they later had to return it to the Israelites (I Sam. 4-7).

In patriarchal times the father of the household offered prayer and sacrifices on behalf of himself and his household, but with the establishment of the covenant between Yahweh and his people at Sinai, a specific priestly tribe was set apart to care for the spiritual ministry in Israel. The priests served as mediators between God and man. They officiated at the offerings (Exod. 28:1-43) and, as custodians of the Law, were expected to instruct the people concerning their moral and cultic obligations. By means of Urim and Thummim (Num. 27:1; Deut.

33:8) they sought to discern Yahweh's will and make it known
to the people. The priests were to be examples of holy living,
and they were expected to be particularly careful in matters
of marriage and family discipline (Lev. 21:1 — 22:10).

The priests wore vestments which became the external mark
of their office. The basic garment was a long, white, seamless
tunic over which they wore a girdle of blue, purple, and scarlet
needlework. Breeches of fine linen and a plain, close fitting cap
completed the attire of the ordinary priest (Exod. 28:40-43;
39:27-29). The High Priest wore an additional robe, blue in
color, extending from his neck to below his knees. Attached
to the bottom of the robe was a fringe of alternating bells and
pomegranites.

The High Priestly ephod consisted of two pieces of linen,
gold, blue, purple, and scarlet in color, joined with shoulder
straps. On each shoulder piece was a stone with the names of
six of the twelve tribes. Golden borders and chains of gold
further adorned the ephod. Linked to the shoulder straps of the
ephod was a nine square inch pouch, suspended on chains of
pure gold. This formed the breastplate, in which were set
twelve stones bearing the names of the twelve Israelite tribes.
As his headdress the High Priest wore a turban which bore a
golden plate with the words, "Holiness to the Lord."

In a solemn ceremony the sons of Aaron were set apart for
their priestly work. The consecration ceremony began with a
ceremonial washing in water, after which the future priests were
clothed in the appropriate garments. Moses officiated at the
service in which the subjects were anointed with oil, symbolic
of their induction into the priesthood. Moses then offered a
young ox as a Sin Offering, followed by rams for the Burnt
Offering and the Peace Offering. Then sacrificial blood was
applied to the right thumb, right ear, and the large toe of the
right foot of the priest.

Next Moses took the fat and right leg of his sacrificial victims, along with three pieces of pastry normally alotted to the
priest, and presented them to Aaron's sons for a Wave Offering.
The breasts were presented as Wave Offerings, then boiled and
eaten by Moses and the priests. Before the meal Moses sprinkled
anointing oil and blood on the priests and their garments. The
ceremony was repeated on each of seven days (Exod. 29:1-37;
40:12-15; Lev. 8:1-36).

8

IN THE WILDERNESS

The encampment at Sinai came to an end when the cloud which symbolized God's presence among His people moved northeastward from Mount Sinai. The people followed as far as the Wilderness of Paran (Num. 10:12), a high plateau region composed chiefly of limestone formations. The interminable wastes of Paran are occasionally broken by refreshing oases. Soon after their arrival, the Israelites murmured in disgust against Moses, their leader, remembering the food which they had while in Egypt (Num. 11:1-10). When Moses brought the problem to Yahweh, he was instructed to gather together seventy elders who would share his gift of prophecy and thus aid in administering the affairs of Israel (Num. 11:16-30). When quails were driven into the Wilderness of Paran by a strong wind the people feasted on this delicacy which was a welcome change from the manna which they had come to loathe. No sooner had they begun to eat the quails, however, than a plague broke out in the camp and many died (Num. 11:31-35). The place was named Kibroth-Hattaavah, "graves of craving" because there the people had despised God's provision for their needs and lusted after other food.

Another crisis arose when Miriam and Aaron criticized Moses for marrying an Ethiopian (Heb. "Cushite") woman (Num. 12:1). If the term is taken to mean an Ethiopian, then she was probably one from among the mixed multitude which left Egypt with Israel at the time of the Exodus. Josephus (Antiquities ii.10) preserves a tradition that Moses as commander-in-chief of the Egyptian army had beseiged an Ethiopian city. According to this legend a princess, Tarbis, fell in love with the Hebrew commander and they were married. The story has no historical value but it illustrates the way in which a Jewish historian of the first century A.D. attempted to solve the problem.

Cushite may, however, in this context be derived from Kushu, or Cushan, a tribe associated with Midian (Hab. 3:7). According to the latter hypothesis she was of a tribe closely allied to the people of Jethro and Zipporah. Zipporah was last mentioned after the defeat of Amalek (Exod. 18) and she may have died before Moses took the Ethiopian or Cushite wife. Otherwise Moses had two wives.

The anger of Yahweh was aroused against Miriam and Aaron for speaking against Moses. In punishment for her rebellion, Miriam became leprous and was shut up outside the camp for a week (Num. 12:10-15). Whatever others might think of Moses' marriage, Yahweh made it clear that the lawgiver had done right.

On the northern border of the Wilderness of Paran is Kadesh-barnea, often identified with cAin Qudeis, about fifty miles southwest of Beersheba. Actually the springs at cAin Qudeirat, twelve miles northwest of cAin Qudeis afford much better facilities for an encampment such as that of the Israelites, and modern scholarship suggests that the Israelites encamped in that region, using all of the springs in the area. cAin Qudeirat is the richest spring in northern Sinai flowing between two mountain ranges and irrigating a fertile valley.

Kadesh-barnea served as the headquarters for the Israelite tribes for thirty-eight years (cf. Deut. 2:14). At the beginning of that period Moses chose one man from each of the twelve tribes to go on a spying expedition northward to the land of Canaan. The spies were instructed to survey the land itself, observe the people and note the fortifications (Num. 13:1-20). The spies did as they were told, and returned with enthusiastic reports. It was indeed a land of milk and honey, and they brought a sample of its fruit to back up their glowing report (Num. 13:26-27). While all agreed that the land was all they had hoped for, the majority were so frightened by the walled cities and their powerful defenders that they were not willing to move into Canaan. Caleb, however, urged the people to go up to possess the land, assured that with God's help they could do the otherwise impossible (Num. 13:30). The majority prevailed, however, and a generation of pilgrims became wanderers in the wilderness.

The aftermath of the report of the spies was tragic. The people of Israel seemed to be in a hopeless position, unable to return to Egypt and unable to press on into Canaan. In despair, they said, "Would that we had died in the land of Egypt! Or would that we had died in this wilderness!" When the people actually planned to choose a leader who would take them back to Egypt, Moses interceded before Yahweh. The wrath of Yahweh was turned from his rebellious people, but he declared that the disobedient people would not live to see the promised land (Num. 14:20-25). Only Caleb and Joshua of the people over twenty who had left Egypt would live to see Canaan — the others would perish in the wilderness (Num. 14:26-35).

A group of Israelites, contrary to Moses' wishes, made an abortive attack upon the Amalekites and the Canaanites of the Hill Country of southern Judea, but the Israelites had to flee before them (Num. 14:39-44). A confederation of Canaanite cities under the King of Arad was successful in repulsing the Israelite assault. The attack was contrary to God's will and its results were disastrous. Israel would not attempt to enter Canaan again until after the death of Moses.

A further rebellion broke out against Moses when Korah and a company of other Levites challenged his right to rule. Two hundred and fifty leaders in Israel insisted that all of Yahweh's people were holy, and they resented the fact that Moses was acting like a prince in their midst (Num. 16:3, 13). As a further grievance they reminded Moses that he had not brought them into "a land flowing with milk and honey" although they had followed him from such a land with the promise of better things (Num. 16:12-14). There was also a religious issue, for Korah and the Levites were offended that Aaron's family had been set apart for the privilege of priesthood (Num. 16:8-10).

The revolt came to an end when "the earth opened its mouth and swallowed them up" (Num. 26:9) so that the rebels and their households were destroyed.

The day after Korah and his company had met their death in the awful judgment of Yahweh, the people again complained against Moses for being responsible for the death of their brethren (Num. 16:41). The wrath of Yahweh was again aroused, and fourteen thousand seven hundred people died in a plague (Num. 16:49). As a visual demonstration of God's choice for the priestly office, Moses asked that rods — symbols of authority — be brought by the several tribes. The twelve rods were then deposited in the Tabernacle, and the next day Moses entered the Tabernacle and found that the rod of Aaron "had

The Wilderness near Ezion-geber. Israel's journey to Ezion-geber took her through this barren, mountainous terrain.   Courtesy, Consulate General of Israel

sprouted and put forth buds and produced blossoms, and it bore ripe almonds" (Num. 17:1-11). In this way the appointment of Aaron was confirmed before all Israel.

Miriam, Moses' sister, died while Israel was encamped at Kadesh (Num. 20:1). She was some years older than Moses, for it is generally agreed that Miriam was the sister who watched the baby Moses in the bulrushes and suggested her mother as his nurse. There is no record that she ever married, although rabbinical tradition says that she was Caleb's wife and the mother of Hur.

When the people again murmured for lack of water, Yahweh instructed Moses to speak to the rock, telling it to yield its water (Num. 20:8). Instead, Moses angrily said to the people, "Hear now, ye rebels, shall we bring forth water for you out of this rock?" Thereupon he took his rod and struck the rock twice. Although he was successful in providing water by that means, Yahweh reprimanded him for his disobedience: "Because you did not believe in me to sanctify me in the eyes of the people of Israel, therefore you shall not bring this assembly into the land which I have given them" (Num. 20:12). Moses, like others of his generation, was destined to die without entering the promised land.

Had Israel accepted the counsel of Caleb and Joshua, her armies would have entered Canaan from the south. Instead she passed a generation in the wilderness, after which she revised her military plans. Canaan would be entered from the east, with a crossing of the Jordan north of the Dead Sea in the region of Jericho. The shortest means of doing this was for the Israelites to go around the southern extremity of the Dead Sea, then through Edomite territory northward to the plains of Moab. From Kadesh, Moses sent a request to the king of Edom, urging him to allow his "brother Israel" to pass through his land up the King's Highway, the direct road running from the Gulf of Aqabah to Syria (Num. 20:14-21). Although the Israelites promised to remain on the road and to pay for any water they would consume, the Edomites refused them permission to travel through their country.

Moses and his people turned southeastward from Kadesh, however, and as they approached the border of Edom, Aaron died and was buried at Mount Hor (Num. 20:22-29). Josephus (Antiquities iv. 4. 7) suggests that it was near Petra, and tradition identifies it with a 4,800 foot peak to the west of Edom. Benno Rothenberg, however, locates Mount Hor on the route from Kadesh-barnea to Arad. Near a holy mountain in the vicinity of Tell Arad is the Wadi Harunia which may preserve the name of Mount Hor.

From Mount Hor, Israel began her long detour around Edom (Num. 21:4), turning southeastward toward Ezion-geber on the Gulf of Aqaba, the eastern extension of the Red Sea.

While in the neighborhood of Mount Hor, a Canaanite king of Arad in the Judean Negeb attacked Israel and took some captives (Num. 21:1). Israel was able to make a counter attack and to destroy the Canaanites of the region.

The people again grew impatient at the delays, and again they complained to Moses about their lack of adequate food and water supplies. This time they encountered a plague of venomous serpents whose bite caused painful inflammation and many people died (Num. 21:6-9). When the people acknowledged their sin and sought mercy, Yahweh commanded Moses

The Gulf of Aqaba (right background). Archaeologist
Nelson Glueck is seen reading the Bible to members of
his expedition. They are seated on a hilltop overlooking
the Gulf of Aqaba.   Photo Courtesy, Nelson Glueck

to set up a bronze figure of a serpent on a pole, that those bitten might look to it in faith and live.

Israel made its way northward toward Moab, avoiding the Edomite strongholds as she journeyed (Num. 21:10-20). From Ezion-geber she probably advanced through the Arabah Valley as far as the Zered, which enters the Dead Sea at its tip. Going eastward through the Zered Valley, Israel sought to by-pass Moab. She probably turned northward at the edge of the desert, and then westward through the Arnon Gorge which formed the northern boundary of Moab. North of the Arnon was the Amorite territory of Sihon. Israel asked Sihon for permission to use that portion of the King's Highway that went through his country, and he, like Edom, refused. This time, however, there was a battle. Sihon attacked Israel, but Israel gained a decisive victory and took possession of his land from the Arnon Valley, its southern border, to its northern border on the Brook Jabbok (Num. 21:21-32).

The victory over Sihon gave the Israelite armies courage and they went farther north to the territory of Og, king of Bashan. In a battle at Edrei, Og met defeat at the hand of Israel (Num. 21:33-35). The victories over Sihon and Og in Transjordan were to have important consequences. Word of the power of Israel quickly spread throughout the area and counter measures were attempted.

Balak of Moab, fearing that conventional methods of warfare might prove ineffective, sought the help of a foreign seer named Balaam who had gained a reputation for the potency of his spells. Balaam's home was at Pethor, evidently another form of the name Pitru, a city in the Euphrates Valley near Carchemesh (Num. 22:5; 23:7). Balak wanted Balaam to place a curse upon Israel, but the seer refused to accompany the first group of messengers who sought to purchase his services (Num. 22:7-14). Balak was not discouraged, however. He sent a larger delegation composed of princes of his realm, and finally Balaam was induced to accompany them to Moab.

Balaam did not curse Israel, however. Balak took him to a succession of heights from which he could look upon the Israelite encampment. Instead of uttering curses, however, Balaam pronounced a series of blessings. From the heights overlooking Israel, Balaam spoke of Israel's pre-eminence (Num. 24). Among his prophetic utterances he declared:

I see him, but not now; I behold him but not nigh:
A star shall come forth out of Jacob, and a scepter shall rise out of Israel.

Both Jewish and Christian scholars have seen in these words the promise of a coming Messiah who would come from Israel and bring blessing to mankind. The Jewish nationalist leader who defied Rome in the days of Hadrian (A.D. 132-135) was popularly called Bar Kochba, "son of the star." A star heralded the birth of Jesus to the eastern Magi (Matt. 2:2, 9-10) and the resurrected Christ identified himself in the Revelation as "the root and offspring of David, the bright morning star" (Rev. 22:16).

Scripture does not remember Balaam for the prophecies which he reluctantly uttered, but rather for his base desire for gain (II Peter 2:15). He stands as the example of one with God-given abilities who is ready to sell them to the highest bidder. Although restrained by God from cursing Israel by his utterances, it was at his suggestion (Num. 31:16) that the Moabites invited Israel to participate in the licencious worship at Baal-peor which had terrifying results for Israel. Baal, the Canaanite fertility god was worshiped by rites of religious prostitution in which acts which produce human fertility were thought to symbolically transfer power to the earth, causing it to produce. It was to such an orgy that Israel was invited, and the prior warnings against conformity to the religious standards of Canaan went unheeded (Num. 25:3). Baal-peor marks the beginning of that tendency toward idolatry among the Israelites that continued until the destruction of Jerusalem and the exile that followed. Balaam's counsel was fiendishly successful. Israel sinned, and Yahweh's anger was aroused against the people who had earlier vowed to place no other gods before him. Those who had taken part in the Baal-peor worship were killed and in the plague that followed the incident twenty-four thousand people died (Num. 25:4-9).

After the plague, and toward the close of the thirty-eight years in the wilderness, Moses and Eleazar instructed the people to take a census. Those twenty years of age and older numbered 601,730 (Num. 26:2, 51), as compared with 603,550 at the time of the earlier census taken at Sinai (Num. 1:46). These figures do not include the Levites, of whom there were 23,000 in the census taken at Shittim (Num. 26:62). The purpose of the census was twofold. Since major battles were ahead, it was necessary to ascertain the number of available fighting men. Equally important, since Israel would soon enter the land of Canaan, a basis had to be determined for the equitable division of the land (cf. Num. 26:52-56). The generation that had left

Egypt forty years earlier was dead (Num. 26:63-65), and the new generation would soon possess the land which had been promised to the Biblical patriarchs.

The large numbers of people who died during the wilderness journey caused the survivors to face serious problems concerning inheritance rites. One of these pertained to the daughters of a man named Zelophehad who left no male heirs. His five daughters argued that their father had not participated in the rebellion which Korah led. Had he done so, there would have been no reason to preserve his family's name in Israel. Since he died a "natural death" — the Bible says "for his own sin" (Num. 27:3), implying that all men so die — his daughters felt that they should inherit their father's property. In general, women did not inherit property in a tribal society, but in this instance Moses saw the justice of their plea and ordered that their father's inheritance should go to them (Num. 27:1-11). From that time on the law of inheritance affirmed that an inheritance should pass to daughters when no sons survive.

As Moses approached the end of his life he consecrated Joshua the son of Nun as his successor (Num. 27:12-23). Joshua was a young man at the time of the Exodus (Exod. 33:11) and had distinguished himself in fighting the nomadic Amalekites (Exod. 17:8-13). He represented his tribe, Ephraim, when the spies conducted their survey of the Promised Land, and stood with Caleb in insisting that Israel should trust God and enter their inheritance (Num. 14:6-10). Joshua may have been about seventy years of age when he succeeded Moses as leader of the twelve tribes of Israel.

The death of Moses marks the end of the trek from Egypt to Canaan. After blessing his people (Deut. 33), the aged lawgiver went up from the plains of Moab to Mount Pisgah "which is opposite Jericho" (Deut. 34:1). From that vantage point he could see the Promised Land spread out at his feet, but Moses did not live to enter Canaan. At the age of one hundred twenty he died in Moab, leaving Joshua with the challenge to enter and possess the land which Yahweh had promised to the Patriarchs of Israel.

Mount Nebo in Moab. From the heights of Nebo, Moses could view western Palestine although he did not personally enter the Promised Land. The death of Moses in Moab marked the end of the wilderness wandering. Subsequently Joshua crossed with the Israelites and took the land by conquest.

Courtesy, Matson Photo Service

9

MOSAIC RELIGION

The religion of the Patriarchs had been intensely personal. God appeared to Abraham, Isaac, and Jacob, promising them multiplied progeny (cf. Gen. 15:5) and ultimate inheritance of the land of Canaan (Gen. 13:14-15). By the time of the Exodus, the family had been replaced by the tribe as the self-conscious social unit, but the patriarchal promises were not forgotten. The tribes were returning to the home that God had given them. Joseph, in faith, had refused burial in Egypt, assured that God would one day bring his people back to their homes in Canaan (Gen. 50:24-26). The bones of Joseph which the Israelites took with them when leaving Egypt (Exod. 13:19) provided a link with the Patriarchs and the God who had revealed himself to them.

Under Moses, however, the Israelite tribes took the first steps toward nationhood, and collectively entered into covenant with Yahweh who would henceforth be known in a unique sense as Israel's God. Israel's election was of pure grace. Moses reminded them, "It was not because you were more in number than any other people that Yahweh set his love upon you and chose you, for you were the fewest of all peoples; but it is because Yahweh loves you, and is keeping the oath which he swore to your fathers, that Yahweh has brought you out with a mighty hand, and redeemed you from the house of bondage, from the hand of Pharaoh, king of Egypt" (Deut. 7:7-8).

It was God's purpose that the twelve tribes should develop a national consciousness centered in his revelation. The focus of Old Testament history would henceforth be upon Israel, although the promise that one day all nations would bless themselves in Abraham's seed (Gen. 12:1-2) was never abrogated. Israel had the honored position of the firstborn (Exod. 4:22), but was in no sense the only son.

Yahweh's choice of Israel did not imply that he would bless her under all circumstances. Blessing was conditioned on obedience, and rebellion brought with it strict retribution (cf. Exod. 32:25-29; Num. 11:33; 14:20-38; 17:6-15; 21:6; 25:6-9). Conversely when the heathen obeyed his word, blessing came upon them. The book of Jonah tells how the most wicked city of its day, Nineveh, was spared the wrath of God when it turned to him in penitence. Rahab of Jericho was saved from destruction because she believed in the power of Israel's God and demonstrated her faith by protecting the spies who sought refuge in her house. (Josh. 2).

When God appeared to him in the burning bush (Exod. 3), Moses was concerned that he be able to identify the One who had commissioned him to deliver Israel from Egypt. The Egyptians and their neighbors worshiped many gods, and the Israelites would be expected to question the source of the commission Moses professed to have received from God. God, Hebrew *Elohim,* is a generic name which may be used of the God of Israel or the gods of other peoples. The question of Moses was one of identity: "Who are you?" "How do you identify yourself?"

Many scholars translate God's reply (Exod. 3:14) as a perfect or a future tense of the verb "to be": "I am who I am," "I am what I am," or "I will be what I will be." God would thus be giving a cryptic answer, involving a play on the verb "to be" and the name Yahweh which is derived from that verb. God identified himself to Moses as Yahweh, who had earlier appeared to the Patriarchs (Exod. 3:15).

Israel's God claimed not only to be self-existent but also to be the author of all that exists. The name Yahweh is translated by W. F. Albright,[1] "He causes to be what comes into existence," identifying Israel's God with the Creator and moving power in all things. Israel's neighbors worshiped gods who were identified with the phenomena of nature — sun, moon, River Nile — but Israel's God claimed to be the creator of all things. He showed his control over nature in the plagues which he inflicted upon the rebellious Egyptians (Exod. 7-10), in parting the waters of the Reed Sea (Exod. 15:21) and in providing quails, manna, and water for his people's needs during their long journey. He produced lightning, thunder, and smoke, and

---

1. *From the Stone Age to Christianity* (Garden City, N.Y., Doubleday Anchor Books), pp. 259-261.

caused the very mountains to quake when he gave his Law at
Sinai (Exod. 19:16-19; 20:18).

According to a popular reconstruction of the religion of
Israel, Moses introduced a new deity, or at least a new name
for the deity, to the Israelite tribes after his contacts with
Jethro. Yahweh, adherents to this view claim, was originally a
mountain god worshiped by Kenites and Midianites in the
Sinai peninsula. During Moses' forty years in the wilderness he
is thought to have become a worshiper of Yahweh, whom he
later identified with the God of Israel's Patriarchs. There is no
a priori reason why Jethro might not have known the true
God before his contacts with Moses, as Melchizedek (Gen. 14)
did before the visit of Abraham, but the book of Exodus makes
it clear that the history and religion of the Mosaic era is a con-
tinuation of that of the Patriarchs. Changes affect the externals
of religion, but its essence is the same in Mosiac and Patriarchal
ages.

Another view, popularized by Sigmund Freud, would derive
Mosaic monotheism from the solar monotheism of Akhenaton,
the rebel Pharaoh who renounced the traditional Egyptian
polytheism and devoted himself to the worship of Aton, the
sun disk. While most scholars will agree that Akhenaton's theology was an advancement over that of his predecessors, his reforms were short lived, and their influence on succeeding generations seems to have been slight. Even if Moses had heard of
Akhenaton's reforms, he showed no sympathy for sun worship.
To Israel, all the gods of Egypt — including Aton — were defeated by Yahweh in the events associated with the Exodus.

The God who revealed himself through Moses to Israel forbade the use of images or pictures. As One who is in essence
Spirit, he insisted that no attempt be made to depict him in
the likeness of any created object (Exod. 20:4). He might appear to men in any form he chose, but his Person was not to
be confused with his manifestations. He appeared to Moses in
a flame of fire (Exod. 3:2) and went before his people in the
wilderness in a pillar of cloud by day, and a pillar of fire by
night (Exod. 13:21-22).

Yahweh consistently presents himself to Israel as a holy God
upon whose Person mortal man could not look and live (Exod.
33:20). Even Moses covered his face in God's presence (Exod.
3:6). As a holy God, he demanded holiness of those who worship him (Exod. 19:6). When Nadab and Abihu dishonored
God's holiness they died (Lev. 10:1-3).

The power of Yahweh was demonstrated in the wonders which Moses wrought in Egypt, and in the act of Israel's deliverance. God's power provided sustenance for Israel during its years in the wilderness, and when Moses himself questioned God's ability to meet an extremity, Yahweh asked him, "Is Yahweh's hand shortened?" (Num. 11:23). The seer Balaam tried to curse Israel at the instigation of Balak of Moab, but the power of Yahweh turned his curse into a blessing. When Balak reprimanded Balaam for not following directions, the seer answered, "Must I not take heed to speak what Yahweh puts in my mouth?" (Num. 23:12).

In no sense is Yahweh restricted as to place. He hears the cry of his persecuted people in Egypt and calls Moses in the wilderness to become their deliverer. The Holy of Holies in the sacred Tabernacle is his throne room, but from the highest heaven he smells the sweet-smelling savor of sacrifices offered by the penitent. He is the God of Mount Sinai, but leads his people to Canaan, the land of their inheritance.

No Israelite could question the extent of God's knowledge. He knew of the affliction of his people, but he also knew of Pharaoh's intentions: "I know that the king of Egypt will not let you go unless compelled by a mighty hand" (Exod. 3:19). Yahweh anticipated Pharaoh's every move, and in announcing the last plague said to Moses, "Afterwards he will let you go hence; when he lets you go he will drive you away completely" (Exod. 11:1). Through prophets, God could foretell events of the future (cf. Num. 24:15-24), and through the mysterious Urim and Thummim the High Priest could declare God's will to leaders (Num. 27:21) and people (Deut. 33:8, 10).

The Urim and Thummim were kept in the breastplate of the High Priest (Exod. 28:30; Lev. 8:8) which was attached to the ephod, a garment which reached from the breast to the hips, held in place by two shoulder bands and tied around the waist (Exod. 39:1-26). The inquirer asked questions which could be answered, "Yes" or "No." An answer could not be forced, however. When Saul sought information concerning the impending battle at Mount Gilboa, the Urim gave him no answer (I Sam. 28:6).

The exact nature of the Urim and Thummim is not known, but it has been suggested that they were flat stones, each of which had one side marked Urim (from 'arar, "to curse") and the other marked Thummim (from tamam, "to be perfect"). The stones were either thrown or ceremonially drawn by the priest from the pouch. When both stones displayed the Urim side, a negative answer was given, when both stones showed the Thummim, the answer was positive, and when one Urim and one Thummim appeared, no reply could be given to the question.

Yahweh is consistently presented as a God who is just in his ways, judging the Egyptians when they resist his will, but also judging disobedient and rebellious Israel. Although Balaam as a prophet uttered God's message, the fact that he sought to help Balak in cursing Israel brought divine judgment on his head (Num. 31:8, 16). God's judgments are just, but he delights in mercy. Yahweh describes himself as "a God merciful and gracious, slow to anger and abounding in steadfast love and faithfulness, keeping steadfast love for thousands, forgiving iniquity and transgression and sin, but who will by no means clear the guilty, visiting the iniquity of the fathers upon the children and the children's children to the fourth generation" (Exod. 34:6-7). Yahweh showed his love to Israel by carrying her "on eagles' wings" (Exod. 19:4) to himself.

The mercy of Yahweh is particularly shown in the provision of the Tabernacle, or "Tent of Meeting," at which the sinner could present his offering and receive pardon. He who had spoken amidst the thunderings and lighting of Sinai, directed the sinner to come with a sacrifice to the door of the Tent of Meeting (Lev. 1:1-3). The sanctity of the Tabernacle with its provision that no Israelite save the High Priest, and he only once a year, might enter the Holy of Holies stressed the holiness and inaccessibility of Israel's God. The sacrificial system, the Altar of Burnt Offering at the gate of the Tabernacle, and the laver for the cleansing of the priests, emphasize the corresponding truth — the all-holy God delights in showing mercy to his penitent people.

Although sacrifices had existed from the beginnings of Biblical history (cf. Gen. 4:1-7), they were codified for the first time in the Mosaic legislation. Four kinds of sacrifice involving bloodshed are mentioned in the book of Leviticus: Burnt Offerings, Peace Offerings, Sin Offerings, and Trespass Offerings. The animals had to be ceremonially clean, and offerings were limited to such animals as the Israelites themselves were permitted to eat. These included sheep, goats, and oxen. In certain of the sacrifices either male or female animals might be offered, and in case of poverty, pigeons might be substituted for the more expensive animals.

When sacrifices were made on behalf of the nation, the High Priest officiated. Individuals, however, might bring their own sacrifices to the Altar of Burnt Offering, place their hands on the head of the victim, and kill it. An officiating priest would then sprinkle the blood and burn the sacrifice.

In the Burnt Offering the entire sacrifice was consumed upon the altar (Lev. 1:5-17; 6:8-13), signifying the complete consecration of the offering (cf. Rom. 12:1). The Peace Offering was voluntarily given (Lev. 3:1-17; 7:11-34), and emphasized concepts of communion or fellowship. The fat of the Peace Offering was burned, a part of the remaining meat was assigned to the priest, and the worshiper and his guests feasted on the rest. Atonement for sins committed unwittingly was made through the Sin Offering (Lev. 4:1-35; 6:24-30), and trespasses in which the offender might make restitution were provided for in the Trespass Offering which insisted that the offender repay his debt with an additional double tithe (Lev. 5:14 — 6:7).

Besides the animal sacrifices, provision was made for a Meal Offering (A.V. "Meat Offering," R.S.V. "Cereal Offering") which often accompanied the Burnt Offerings or the Peace Offerings. The offering might be of fine flour mixed with oil, frankincense, and salt, or of flour prepared in the oven in the form of bread, cakes, or wafers (Lev. 2:1-16; 6:14-23). Honey was rigidly excluded from the Meal Offerings.

Before the giving of the law at Sinai, the Sabbath was set apart as a day of solemn rest (Exod. 16:22-30). Festivities also marked the beginning of each month (the "new moon," Num. 10:10) and, in particular, the beginning of the seventh month which was known in Old Testament times as the Feast of Trumpets (Lev. 23:23-25; Num. 28:11-15; 29:1-6). The Passover Feast, commemorating the Exodus, was associated with the Feast of Unleavened Bread which immediately followed it (Exod. 10:2; 12:8, 14; Num. 28:16-25). As an agricultural festival it commemorated the beginning of the barley harvest, but its prime religious interest centered in the celebration of deliverance from Egyptian bondage. Fifty days after the Passover, Israel celebrated another agricultural festival, marking the beginning of the wheat harvest. This festival, known in the Old Testament as the Feast of Weeks (Exod. 23:16; 34:22) was later known as Pentecost (Acts 2). Prescribed offerings were presented to Yahweh, and Israel was reminded of the necessity of remembering the poor (Lev. 23:22).

The tenth day of the Seventh month was the Day of Atonement, the most solemn day of the year (Exod. 30:10; Lev. 16:1-34; 23:26-31). In elaborate ceremonies, propitiation was made for Aaron and his sons, for the Holy Place itself, for the Tent of Meeting, for the Altar of Burnt Offering, and for the whole people of Israel. It was on the Day of Atonement that the High Priest entered the Most Holy Place to perform his sacred rite of sprinkling blood. In another of the colorful rituals of the day, two goats were set apart as a Sin Offering for the people. The High Priest sacrificed one goat at the altar, then he put his hand on the head of the live goat and confessed Israel's sins. The goat was then taken into the wilderness to carry away the sins of the people. The concept of the goat that escaped into the wilderness gives us our word "scapegoat."

From the fifteenth to the twenty-second day of the seventh month, Israel observed the Feast of Booths, or Tabernacles (Exod. 23:14-17), the final holy days of the year. The Israelites actually lived in booths made of the boughs of trees or palm tree branches during the week, remembering the period of wandering in the wilderness when such temporary abodes served as dwelling places for the people (Lev. 23:43).

In addition to the weekly sabbath, the sabbath principle was applied to years (Exod. 23:10-11). The land was to lie fallow every seventh year (Lev. 25:2-5), after six years of sowing, pruning, and harvesting. Natural growth from the field might be gleaned by the poor, and anything left was for the beasts (Exod. 23:11; Deut. 15:2-18). In the Sabbatical Year any Hebrew who was in bondage to another was to be set free (cf. Jer. 34:14) and creditors were instructed to cancel debts incurred by the poor during the six previous years (Deut. 15:1-11).

After seven sabbatical cycles, the fiftieth year was known as the Jubilee. It was observed like sabbatical years, with the additional provision that property revert to its original owners, debts be remitted, and Hebrews who were enslaved for debt be released. The Jubilee was a time of thanksgiving and genuine rejoicing. The American Liberty Bell which proclaimed the birth of our nation from Independence Hall, Philadelphia, bears the inscription from Leviticus 25:10 describing the significance of the Jubilee: "Proclaim liberty throughout all the land to all the inhabitants thereof."

The concept of justice in Israel is illustrated by provision made for six Cities of Refuge to be designated after the conquest of Canaan (Num. 35:9-28). Three would be located on each side of the Jordan as asylums to which a fugitive man-slayer might flee. The man who had killed another accidentally was allowed to stay in the City of Refuge until the death of the High Priest. There he would be protected from the relatives of the deceased who would otherwise seek revenge. A wilful murderer, however, was not granted asylum, but was surrendered to the avenger and put to death.

The provision that the accidental homicide could remain in a City of Refuge until after the death of the High Priest was interpreted in later Jewish writings as a vicarious expiation of life for life. After the death of the High Priest the manslayer was free to leave the City of Refuge and his person was then regarded as safe. The demand for blood revenge was satisfied by the priest's death.

Machtesh Ramon in the Negeb. This may be Biblical Rimmon-perez (Num. 33:19) one of the Israelite camping grounds during the years of wandering after leaving Kadesh (Num. 14:25).   Photo Courtesy, Nelson Glueck

10

DATES AND FIGURES

In our age of scientific calculations we may grow somewhat impatient at ancient methods of reckoning. Worse yet, we may assume that the Biblical writers used the same rules that we do for historical writing, and judge them harshly when their results do not tally with our expectations. Scholars have long puzzled over the date of the Exodus, and the number of people who left Egypt with Moses — two problems which reflect the use of figures by Biblical writers.

It should be clear to all who read the Book of Exodus, that dates and names which can be compared with known Egyptian history form no part of the Biblical record. The ruler is simply "Pharaoh" — the word used for any Egyptian king. Modern scholars may argue concerning the identity of the Pharaoh of the oppression and the Pharaoh of the Exodus, but the Biblical writer was not interested in supplying that information. To be sure, the identification of these individuals would help us to place Biblical history in its contemporary setting, but we must remember that the Bible itself does not identify them.

It may be argued, however, that the Bible does provide material for an exact chronology. In I Kings 6:1 we read, "In the four hundred and eightieth year after the people of Israel came out of the land of Egypt, in the fourth year of Solomon's reign over Israel . . . he began to build the house of the Lord." Since the fourth year of Solomon's reign was about 960 B.C., a simple mathematical solution would suggest that the Exodus took place around 1440 B.C., a date which is defended by some modern scholars. Thutmose III was the Pharaoh at that time. Although he, like the Pharaoh who oppressed the Israelites, was famous for building operations in which slave labor was employed, Thutmose III resided at Thebes in Upper Egypt, while the Pharaoh whose daughter found the infant Moses, and the

Pharaoh to whom Moses went with the demand that Israel be released, lived in the eastern Delta, near the land of Goshen. In fact one of the store cities upon which the Israelites labored is named Raamses, evidently the Egyptian Per-Raamses, "the house of Rameses," named for Rameses II. Although this may be a modernized form of an older name, other evidence suggests that Rameses II may have been the Pharaoh who oppressed the Israelites. Nelson Glueck's explorations in Transjordan suggest that Edom and Moab developed into powerful kingdoms defended by border fortifications about 1300 B.C. Had the Israelites sought to pass through these lands prior to 1300 B.C. there would presumably have been no powerful government to impede their progress. The fact that Pharaohs of the Rameside Age had capitals in the eastern Delta at Tanis, which is probably to be identified with Raamses, harmonizes well with the Biblical descriptions of the relations between the Pharaohs and the Israelites in the Book of Exodus.

The four hundred eighty years of I Kings 6:1 has variants, although they do not assist in computing dates. Several of the better Septuagint manuscripts (B and A) read "four hundred and forty years," and Josephus gives "five hundred ninety two years."[1] Josephus probably arrived at his calculations by adding up the figures in the books of Judges, Samuel and Kings. He erred in assuming that such figures were all successive when in reality some are contemporaneous. In all probability Judges overlapped one another in various parts of the country.

Bible students have long been aware that the figure 40 and its multiples appears very frequently in the earlier books of the Bible. Solomon and David each reigned forty years. The judgeships of Eli, Deborah and Barak, Gideon, and Othniel were each forty years, that of Ehud, eighty years. Israel spent forty years in the wilderness until the generation that left Egypt (except for Caleb and Joshua) had died. In this usage forty years appears to be a conventional way of saying a generation, and the four hundred eighty years from the Exodus to Solomon may represent twelve generations.

Such considerations lead us to conclude that we do not have in our Biblical texts for the period before the Israelite monarchy sufficient data to enable us to establish an absolute chronology. If other considerations within the Biblical text suggest the possibility of a date other than 1440 B.C. for the date

---

1. *Antiquities* vii. 3. 1.

of the Exodus, there is no reason for insisting, on the basis of I Kings 6:1, that they should not be carefully considered.

We do know that Israelites were in Canaan by the last quarter of the thirteenth century. A stele of Pharaoh Merneptah, erected about 1200 B.C. mentions Israel by name among the Palestinian peoples defeated by the Egyptians:

> The princes are prostrate, saying, "Mercy!"
> Not one raises his head among the Nine Bows.
> Desolation is for Tehenu; Hatti is pacified;
> Plundered is the Canaan with every evil;
> Carried off is Ashkelon; seized upon is Gezer;
> Yanoam is made as that which does not exist;
> Israel is laid waste, his seed is not;
> Hurru is become a widow for Egypt!
> All lands together, they are pacified;
> Everyone who was restless, he has been bound.

Archaeological expeditions at Bethel, Lachish, and Debir in Palestine have produced evidence that these cities fell as a result of violent attack some time between 1250 and 1200 B.C. John Garstang's earlier work at Jericho had convinced him that he had discovered Joshua's wall, and that it fell around 1400 B.C., lending support to the early date of the Exodus. More recent studies at Jericho by Kathleen Kenyon suggest that Garstang was mistaken. The wall which he associated with Joshua was really several centuries older than his 1400 B.C. date, and the Jericho evidence can no longer be cited in favor of an early date for the Exodus.

According to Exodus 12:40, Israel spent four hundred thirty years in Egypt. If this is taken to mean the entire period from Joseph to Moses, the following chronology may be suggested:

Period of Favor in Egypt	1710-1550 B.C. 15th to 17th Dynasties	Hyksos Rule from Avaris in the Delta
Period of Disfavor in Egypt	1550-1308 B.C. 18th Dynasty	Native Egyptian Rulers expel Hyksos and rule from Thebes in Upper Egypt
Period of the Exodus	1308-1290 B.C. 19th Dynasty	Seti I (1308-1290 B.C.) and Rameses II (1290-1224 B.C.) rule from Tanis (=Avaris) in the Delta.

The above figures presuppose a date for the Exodus around 1290 B.C.[2] The reference in Exodus 12:40 may be interpreted as dealing solely with the years of oppression (cf. Gen. 15:13), yielding a much longer period for the sojourn of Israel in Egypt.

---

2. Based on the reconstruction suggested by Bernhard W. Anderson, *Understanding the Old Testament* (Englewood Cliffs, N.J.: Prentice Hall, 1960), pp. 26-30.

Conversely, the Greek Septuagint reads that Israel lived in Egypt and Canaan for four hundred thirty years, thus reckoning the whole period from Abraham to Moses as approximately four centuries. Paul, in Galatians 4:13-17, speaks of the Law as given four hundred and thirty years after God's covenant with Abraham. In Stephen's speech, four hundred years is mentioned as the period of oppression (Acts 7:6, based on Gen. 15:13).

If we add the four hundred thirty years of Exodus 12:40 to the 1290 B.C. date for the Exodus we have 1720 B.C. for the entrance of Israel into the land of Egypt. Israel recollected a relationship to the "Era of Tanis" in the note that Hebron was built "seven years before Zoan [=Tanis] in Egypt" (Num. 13:22). The fact that Israel dated events from the era of Tanis suggests relations with the rulers who established Tanis (Avaris) as their delta capital.

Some time during the reign of Horemhab (*ca.* 1340 — *ca.* 1303 B.C.), a stele was erected at Tanis commemorating the four hundredth anniversary of the city which evidently was founded around 1700 B.C. By that time the Hyksos were well established in Egypt, and it is probably they who built Zoan-Tanis as their capital in the eastern Delta.

As perplexing as the problem of the date of the Exodus, is the question of the number of participants. In round figures the Biblical text mentions six hundred thousand male Israelites (Exod. 12:37), to which wives, children, and members of the "mixed multitude" of hangers-on must be added. On that basis the total number can hardly have been fewer than two million. Biblical scholars have hesitated to posit so large a figure for a variety of reasons. So large a company could have been enslaved by Pharaoh only with the greatest difficulty, and Pharaoh's attempts to control them would involve staggering expenditures in manpower. The greatest battle during the reign of Rameses II saw but four divisions, 20,000 men, in the field according to Egyptian records.

The logistics of moving two million people across the Reed Sea in one night are themselves staggering. We must not, of course, picture the Israelites marching in columns through the Sinai Peninsula. Alois Musil, a Czech explorer, has noted the movements of modern nomads, which may give some indication of the way the Israelites traveled. As many as five thousand families may migrate at one time, moving in a column three miles deep and twelve miles wide. The wider the line, the greater the amount of available pasture, but also the greater the risk of groups lagging behind and being cut off by an enemy. A deeper line will mean less pasture for the families in the rear, but it provided better protection for the group.

Scholars have resorted to numerous expedients in trying to account for the six hundred thousand men mentioned in the traditional text. One expedient is to suggest a scribal error. If six thousand were meant, we might have a total group of 25,000, a figure more like what we would expect under the circumstances. Those who argue for a smaller number note that but two midwives were able to care for the obstetrical needs of all Israel (Exod. 1:15), and the spies at Kadesh-barnea reported that the Israelites could not hope to conquer the more powerful Canaanites (Num. 13). Although Jericho was a major military engagement we read that "about forty thousand ready armed for war passed over before the Lord for battle to the plains of Jericho" (Josh. 4:13).

George E. Mendenhall has sought to resolve the problems by interpreting the word *Elif*, "thousand" as a tribal subunit or grouping.[3] He argues that the lists are authentic ancient records of the contingents sent to war by each of the tribes, and reckons 5,550 fighting men on the basis of Numbers 1, and 5,750 on the basis of Numbers 26.

Some years ago W. F. Albright suggested that the population figures in the Exodus records were actually figures from the census of David (II Sam. 24). The figures in Exodus and Numbers would thus be misplaced census figures. It might be argued that actually all Israel took part in the Exodus — that later Israelites were represented by the generation which pledged allegiance to Yahweh at Sinai.

No solution to the problem has proved entirely satisfactory. Scripture makes it clear that the number of Israelites in the Sinai Peninsula was so large that supernatural provision had to be made to provide sustenance, but that it was small enough for the Egyptians to oppress and for nomadic Amalekites to threaten. Israel gained victories in Transjordan over Sihon and Og, but these victories were attributed to divine intervention rather than to the might of Israel. Jericho fell as a result of a miracle by which the walls fell to permit the invading Israelites to enter and despoil the city. It is an important motif in the story of the Exodus and Conquest that God brought down the mighty foe in order that His people might be preserved and inhabit the land promised to their fathers.

---

3. "The Census Lists of Numbers 1 and 26," *JBL* (LXXVII) (1958), pp. 52-66.

PRIMARY SOURCE MATERIAL

There are no contemporary records of Israel's sojourn in Egypt.
The first mention of Israel in Egyptian literature is
in the Hymn of Victory of Mer-ne-Ptah, translated
by John A. Wilson in: J. B. Pritchard, ed., *Ancient
Near Eastern Texts Relating to the Old Testament*
(Princeton, 1955).

History and Geography of Egypt

Baikie, James, *The Amarna Age* (New York: The Macmillan
Company, 1926).
———, *Egyptian Antiquities in the Nile Valley* (London: Methu-
en and Co., 1932).

Breasted, James H., *A History of Egypt* (New York: Charles
Scribner's Sons, 1909).

Aldred, Cecil, *The Egyptians* (London: Thames and Hudson,
1961).

Gardiner, Alan, *Egypt of the Pharaohs* (Oxford: The Claren-
don Press, 1961).

Kees, Hermann, *Ancient Egypt: A Geographical History of the
Nile* (Chicago: University of Chicago Press, 1961).

Steindorff, George, and Keith C. Seele, *When Egypt Ruled the
East,* 2nd edition (Chicago: University of Chicago
Press, 1957).

Wilson, John A., *The Burden of Egypt,* (Chicago: University
of Chicago Press, 1951).

Hayes, W. C., *The Scepter of Egypt* (New York: Harper &
Brothers, 1953).

History of Israel

Bright, John, *A History of Israel* (Philadelphia: Westminster
Press, 1959).

Mallon, Alexis, "Les Hebreux en Egypte," *Orientalia* III (1921), pp. 1-209.

Meek, Theophile J. M., *Hebrew Origins* (rev. ed., New York: Harper Torchbooks, 1960), pp. 1-48.

Peet, T. Eric, *Egypt and the Old Testament* (Liverpool: University Press, 1922).

Rowley, H. H., *From Joseph to Joshua* (London: Oxford University Press, 1950).
———, "Israel's Sojourn in Egypt," *Bulletin of the John Rylands Library*, XXII (1938), pp. 243-290.

Religion of Egypt

Hayes, W. C., "The Religion and Funerary Beliefs in Ancient Egypt," *The Scepter of Egypt*, I, pp. 75-83 (New York: Harper and Brothers, 1953).

Mosaic Religion

Mendenhall, G. E., *Law and Covenant in Israel and the Ancient Near East* (Pittsburgh: The Biblical Colloquium, 1955).

SPECIAL STUDIES

The Sinai Peninsula:

W. F. Albright, "Exploring in Sinai," *Bulletin of the American Schools of Oriental Research*, No. 109 (Feb. 1948), pp. 5-20.
Beno Rothenberg, *God's Wilderness: Discoveries in Sinai* (London, Thames and Hudson, 1961).
C. S. Jarvis, *Yesterday and Today in Sinai*, 1931.
W. M. F. Petrie, *Researches in Sinai* (London).
E. Robinson, *Biblical Researches*, I (11th ed.) 1856.
C. L. Wooley and T. E. Lawrence, *The Wilderness of Zin* (London: Palestine Exploration Fund, 1914).
C. W. Wilson and H. S. Palmer, *Ordnance Survey of the Peninsula of Sinai* (1869-72).

The Nile Delta:
H. Cazelles, "Donnees geographiques sur l'exode," *Revue d'histoire et de philosophie religeuses* (1955), pp. 55.

A. H. Gardiner, "The Delta Residence of the Ramesides," *Journal of Egyptian Archaeology,* V (1918), pp. 127-38, 179-200, 242-71.

————, "The Geography of the Exodus, an answer to Professor Naville and others," *Journal of Egyptian Archaeology* X (1924) pp. 87-96.

————, "The Geography of the Exodus," in *Recueil d'etudes egyptologiques dediees a la memoire de Jean-Francois Champollion* (Paris, 1922) pp. 203-15.

————, "Tanis and Pi-Ramesse: A Retraction," *Journal of Egyptian Archaeology* XIX (1933), pp. 122-8.

Edom and Moab:
Nelson Glueck, *The Other Side of the Jordan* (New Haven: American Schools of Oriental Research, 1940).

Balaam:
William F. Albright, "The Oracles of Balaam," *Journal of Biblical Literature,* LXIII (1944), pp. 207-233.

The Date of the Exodus:
J. W. Jack, *The Date of the Exodus* (Edinburgh, T. & T. Clark, 1925).

C. deWet, *The Date and Route of the Exodus* (London: Tyndale Press, 1960).

The Census Lists:
G. E. Mendenhall, "The Census Lists of Numbers 1 and 26," *Journal of Biblical Literature,* LXXVII (1958), pp. 52-66.

The Tabernacle:
Frank M. Cross, "The Tabernacle," Biblical Archaeologist X (1947), pp. 45-68.

The Manna:
F. S. Bodenheimer, "The Manna of Sinai," *Biblical Archaeologist* X (1947), pp. 2-6.

INDEX

Eliezer, 44
Elim, 54
Elkab, 21
Emmer, 16
Er-raha, 57
Esna, 21
Etham, 52
Euphrates, 18
Ezion-geber, 72

Faiyum, 14, 20
First Cataract, 12, 14
First Intermediate Period, 18
Flax, 17
Fourth Cataract, 12

Geb, 25, 26
Gershom, 44
Golden Calf, 59
Golden Lampstand, 63
Goshen, 17, 34, 35, 36, 41, 47
Great Pyramid, 14

Haᶜapi, 49
Hagar, 52
Hapiru, 36
Hathor, 20, 21, 22, 26
Hebron, 36
Heliopolis, 20, 26, 41 42
Hephaestus, 21
Hermopolis, 21, 26
Herwer, 20
Hittites, 34, 60
Hittite Treaty, 60, 61
Holy of Holies, 64
Hophra, 19
Hor, Mt., 70
Horemhab, 87
Horus, 20, 21, 22, 24, 25
Hurrians, 34
Hyksos, 16, 18, 34, 35

Imhotep, 24
Inundation, 13
Iron, 18
Isis, 22, 26, 29

Jacob, 36
Jambres, 46

Jannes, 46
Jebel Barkal, 12
Jebel Katarin, 57
Jebel Musa, 56, 57
Jebel Serbel, 57
Jericho, 35
Jeroboam, 19
Jethro, 44, 56, 78
Jochebed, 40
Joseph, 13, 16, 20, 33, 34
Joshua, 56, 58, 68, 70, 74
Jubilee Year, 82

Ka, 29
Kadesh-barnea, 67, 69, 88
Karnak, 22
Khenty-Imentiu, 29
Khepri, 25
Khnum, 20, 22, 24, 25, 26
Khonsu, 22
Kibroth-Hattaavah, 66
Korah, 68

Lamb, 49
Levites, 68
Lower Egypt, 14

Maᶜat, 22
Manetho, 34
Manna, 54, 59
Marah, 54
Meal Offering, 81
Mediterranean, 16
Memphis, 11, 13, 18, 20
Menes, 18, 21
Mercy Seat, 64
Merneptah, 33, 53, 86
Middle Kingdom, 18
Midian, 44
Midwives, 38, 39
Migdol, 53
Min, 20, 21, 22
Miriam, 40, 66, 69
Moab, 70, 72, 85
Moeris, Lake, 14
Monotheism 58
Montu, 20, 21
Moses, 40-45, 46-50
Mut, 22, 26